Nelson B. Hairston

I CHOSE CAVIAR

I CHOSE CAVIAR

by

ART BUCHWALD

LONDON
VICTOR GOLLANCZ LTD
1958

First published November 1957
Second Impression Before Publication
Third impression November 1957
Fourth impression November 1957
Fifth impression November 1957
Sixth impression January 1958
Seventh impression January 1958
Eighth impression April 1958
Ninth impression October 1958

Printed in Great Britain by
The Camelot Press Ltd., London and Southampton

CONTENTS

VIVE LE SPORT

A FEW NOTES FROM THE AUTHOR

MOST PEOPLE think the International Set is made up of a group of wealthy party goers who frit away their time in Paris, St. Moritz and on the Riviera. But that's not all they do. Many of us are big-game hunters, beaglers, cricketeers and pigeon-shooters. We mount polo ponies, elephant charges, and Mercedes Benzes. A day doesn't go by when we're not proving ourselves on land, on sea and in the air.

On the following pages you will see how difficult it is to maintain one's position in the International Set. This is a modest record of my accomplishments, perhaps not comparable to the achievements of Aly Khan, Rubi Rubirosa, Captain Townsend and the Duke of Windsor, but I like to think it has got me where I am today—just six seats down from an Elsa Maxwell dinner party, and four stalls down from the Rothschild racing stables.

Despite the fact I never tasted caviar until I was nine years old, I have overcome the handicap by going to the Congo, Lapland, Monaco, Yugoslavia and Dallas, Texas. I have broken bread with Greek shipowners and British Press lords, and recently I played a game of marbles with Lady Docker, one of the great nibs players of England. As this book will prove, there is more to being a playboy than playing around.

It's obvious that most of the people in this book exist in one form or another, but any similarity between these people and other people is purely coincidental. I have tried to make this book as simple as possible so the International Set could read it. But the book is written not solely for them but for all people who aspire to become one of us or who admire what we stand for.

As the Duke of Argyll once said to me: "As far as I'm concerned there are only two kinds of people in the world. Those who are nice to their servants and those who aren't."

The book is dedicated to both kinds.

COWARD AT LARGE

COWARD IN THE CONGO

DEEP DOWN IN every writer lies the horn of the hunter. To most people it may sound like gas on the stomach, but when a writer hears it, he knows Africa is calling. There was a time, many years ago, when to be a writer all you had to do was write. Today if you want to be a writer you have to shoot a big-game animal. You've got to go to the Dark Continent and prove you're a lion among men, a killer of kudu, a butcher in the bush and a fearless fellow in the forest.

While covering the European scene for the New York *Herald Tribune* in recent years I have been insulted by friends and strangers. "Hemingway has killed his leopard," they say. "Ruark has killed his lion. Pray, what have you killed?"

Several summers ago I began to feel the pressure even at home. My wife would never come out and say anything, but I could tell by the little things that all was not going well. Finally, after an unexpected outburst of tears, she told me what was bothering her. "We've been married for more than two years," she said, "and you don't have a trophy to your name. Everyone is laughing at me. They ask me what you do and when I tell them they say, 'If he's a writer, what's the name of his white hunter?'"

I tried to comfort her, but I knew I had failed her. I knew if I wanted our marriage to last I could no longer keep the killer instinct down inside me, next to my ulcer. I could no longer ignore the horn of the hunter.

I picked up the phone and called Sabena Airlines.

"Let me have two tickets to the Congo."

"Why two tickets?" my wife asked.

"You have to come with me to take pictures of my trophies. All the wives do it."

"I'm not going," she said. "I can't stand the sight of your blood. Take Joe Covello. He's a photographer and he can give you moral support. Besides, he'll make a wonderful gin-bearer."

It's funny she should have mentioned Covello. The last I had heard from him, he was in Rome photographing Italian movie stars on leopard skins. He probably knew a great deal about animals by now, and I was sure he would welcome a change. Besides, this safari would give him an opportunity to photograph animals in the flesh, instead of vice versa.

Covello seemed reluctant to leave his work, but he did admit he was running out of leopard skins, and Africa seemed like a good place to replenish his supply.

We flew directly to Stanleyville, our yellow-fever shots tingling in our arms, our eyes glassy from typhoid serum, our hands shaking from the effects of quinine pills. Even before we landed I could hear the native tom-toms beating out a message. "White hunter . . . no guts . . . white hunter . . . no guts."

In Stanleyville we took a taxi to the office of José Ingels & Son, who operate a company called Congo Safari. Ingels is no stranger to the safari business. He took John Huston out in search of wild boar, he took Katharine Hepburn out in search of wild crocodiles and he took Humphrey Bogart out in search of a drink. During the shooting of the movie *The African Queen*, he saw that Lauren Bacall had forty-five bottles of soda-water a day for her bath, and he killed hundreds of mosquitoes on producer Sam Spiegel's back. Ingels was a good man for a tough job.

I stuck out my trigger finger and we shook hands.

"Do you have any safaris for cowards?" I asked Ingels.

"Not at the moment," he replied. "I've got a group of thirty-five Americans, the oldest eighty-seven, who are going to the Albert National Park to take some movies. I could put you on that."

I was about to sign up when Covello reminded me I had to kill an animal.

"Oh, you want to *kill* something," Ingels said, putting on his pith helmet. "Well, you've come to the right place. The Belgian Congo is full of wild game. We can offer anything you want. What about a lion?"

"Is it dangerous?"

"Heavens, no. Except of course if the creature is hiding in the bush, or if you wound him or have to follow him into the dense undergrowth. Or if the female is trying to protect her cubs, or if the lion thinks he's cornered and wants to make a fight of it, or if you attack the male and the female tries to sink her claws in you."

"What else do you have?"

"How about a nice pachyderm? Elephants are great fun, particularly if they know they're being hunted and decide to hunt the hunter. You have to get right up to an elephant to get in a good shot and naturally he'll charge if he sees you. He'll put up his flappy ears and head straight at the man with the gun. If you don't kill him on the first shot it may be your last.

"When he gets on top of you he'll grab you with his trunk and smash you against a tree or the ground. Then he'll either trample on you or gut you with his tusks. Once he thinks you're dead he'll cover you up with leaves or grass. Elephants always give their victims a proper funeral. I must warn you of one thing. It will cost you two hundred dollars for a licence if you want an elephant."

"Two hundred dollars," I said thoughtfully. "That's not too bad, considering you get a burial and everything. But don't you have something a little more my size?"

Ingels measured me around the waist.

"You can try for rhino if you wish, but rhinos usually attack without provocation and there is not much to shoot at, once one is coming towards you. You'll be a big man if you shoot a rhino.

"Then there's always leopard. I'll bet you'd like to bring your wife back a nice leopard coat. Shooting leopards in the Congo is a praiseworthy business and the natives will be grateful if you do it. But leopards are not easy to find. They've been known to hide in trees and jump on you as you walk under them. They'll rip you to bits with their claws. Even if they just scratch you, the poison in their talons can kill you. But they do make wonderful coats."

Ingels ran down the list of other game. He mentioned hartebeest, waterbuck, sassabies, red and black lechwes, Vardon cob, Thomas cob, impala buck, bushbuck, oribis, klipspringer, wart-hogs, Livingston eland, bongos, topis, Neuman cob and scaly anteaters.

"You are not permitted to hunt gorillas," he said. "They are protected by law."

It was the first good news I had heard all day.

Finally it was decided by Ingels and Covello that I would shoot a buffalo. The buffalo is the meanest, most thieving card-cheating, wife-stealing animal in the Congo. But Covello tried to be encouraging. "The buffalo isn't as dangerous as everyone makes him out to be. Statistics prove that in the United States more Americans are killed in automobile accidents than are killed by buffalo."

Ingels arranged to send us out with his son, a strapping twenty-five-year-old lad who would be in charge of our porters, buy our food, take care of our transportation, guns and camping equipment, and tell us true stories of other hunting safaris.

Before we left Stanleyville, Ingels and his son took me to be outfitted. They bought me regulation shorts, a bush jacket, a slouch hat, a toothbrush and a bottle of gin. There was no doubt about it, I was dressed to kill.

We loaded the car with mosquito netting and first-aid equipment and—as is the custom with anyone who is going out hunting for the first time—I was asked to pay Ingels in advance. "The executors of the estate are sometimes reluctant to pay," Ingels explained apologetically.

It is 250 miles as the crow flies from Stanleyville to Irumu. No crow would make it if he went by car. The road twists and turns through the rain-soaked Ituri forest, and the animals, which have a habit of sitting in the middle of the road are neither frightened nor impressed by an automobile horn. The law of the jungle reads that under all conditions an animal has the right of way, and in the few recorded cases where the driver and the animal have both lost their tempers, the animal has always come out on top.

As an added attraction on the safari, we stopped off at a Pygmy camp to take pictures. It cost us only twenty dollars apiece, but the Pygmies warned us if we made any postcards from the photos they wanted royalties on the sales.

In Irumu we found the white hunter. His name was Alex Pierrard and in six years he had bagged more than one hundred elephant, lion, leopard, rhino and python. His walls were jammed with trophies and you couldn't walk on the floor without slipping on an antelope or leopard skin. He had rhino horns for ash trays and elephant tusks for coat racks, and wild boar heads for door-stops. Pierrard was a white hunter to give any yellow hunter confidence.

Young Ingels explained to Pierrard that I was after buffalo, and the white hunter, who noticed that the left side of my face was twitching, looked surprised.

"I can find you all the buffalo you want," Pierrard said. "But are you sure you want to do it? It's pretty risky business, particularly if you've never hunted them before."

"See here, sir," said Covello. "We know it's risky

business and that's why we're out here. If you don't want to take us we'll find another white hunter."

I tried to shut Covello up, but he was very indignant. "It just so happens that my friend here is one of the best shots in Paris. Just because his face is twitching and he's cowering behind your couch is no reason for you to become insulting. My friend wants a buffalo in the worst way and he's determined to pay for it."

Pierrard apologized and said he would arrange porters and would borrow a *tipoye*—a carrying chair for rough travel—as we had a great deal of country to cover. "If it's buffalo you want," he said, "it's buffalo you're going to get."

The next morning we started out bright and early to find a camp. We hired twenty-five porters at twenty cents per head. They were in the truck with the supplies and we followed in a station wagon. Our first inkling that all would not go well on the safari came when the truck, which was being towed on a raft across a fast-moving river, sank to the muddy bottom. We saved the porters and the supplies, but it took us two days to get the truck out of the river. It was heartbreaking work, particularly when I thought about the porters costing me twenty cents a day.

We finally made camp and I was given a tent to myself and my own Gideon Bible. Modern safaris think of everything.

The best part of hunting in Africa is camping out. There —underneath an autumn moon, with a large roaring fire and the companionship of good fellows, large safari ants and malaria-ridden mosquitoes feeding on what little there is left after the scorpions get finished with you—a man is at peace with the world.

Over warm beer and pickled elephant ears, we talked the talk of men—the animals we had shot, the women we had known, the Marilyn Monroe pictures we had seen.

Pierrard cleaned and oiled the guns, Covello and Ingels practiced making tourniquets and splints in case anything went wrong, and the natives argued amongst themselves who was going to draw my bath the next morning.

It was a pleasant evening, and I thought to myself, perhaps for the last time, that it was good to be alive.

The next morning Pierrard and I went out to find my buffalo. The porters carried me for three miles in the *tipoye* and my gun-bearer walked by my side. I had intended to shoot my buffalo from the seat, but Pierrard wouldn't permit it. Besides, if the buffalo charged and the porters ran, I would be caught with my *tipoye* down.

So the white hunter, the beaters, my gun-bearer and I went into the savanna on foot. About seven o'clock we sighted a herd. We dropped down on our bellies and Pierrard indicated it was time to crawl forward. I kept thrashing with my arms and legs but I wasn't going anywhere and finally Pierrard made the beaters pull me along. We got within sixty yards and then Pierrard whispered:

"That's your boy."

He pointed to the largest bull in the herd, the meanest, cruellest hunk of fauna in the entire green hills of Africa. He had horns the size of two curved Eiffel Towers, and a face that would stop Big Ben. His hump was slightly smaller than Mount Everest and each shoulder looked like the front of the *Super Chief*. To top it off he had Native Dancer's legs.

I tried to crawl away but Pierrard held me by the belt.

"Let's forget the whole idea," I whispered. "Live and let live, I always say."

"It's too late now. You better take him. Bust him between the neck and the chest."

I got up on one knee and sighted. I squeezed the trigger slowly.

You think a lot of things when you're about to kill your

first buffalo. You remember a lot of people who have been close to you.

As I squeezed the trigger I thought about the boys at Toots Shor's and how we used to sit around together with Leo Durocher, Joe DiMaggio, Bill O'Dwyer, Bob Considine and Tallulah Bankhead.

I thought about my good friends Leonard Lyons, Earl Wilson and Ed Sullivan and how we used to hunt items together in much darker places than Africa.

I thought about Sherman Billingsley. Good old Sherm. I knew I was going to miss him, even though he used to throw me out of the Stork Club every night. Well, that's not exactly true. He never let me in.

I thought of Elsa Maxwell and what a fine buffalo hunter she would make if only she took it seriously. I thought of Walter Winchell and the many Sunday nights we used to stay up together, he in his radio studio and I in my home in Forest Hills. I fervently wished he and Lenny Lyons would stop feuding.

I kept squeezing the trigger.

I thought of Hedda Hopper and Louella Parsons, who had gone after much bigger game than I had, and had Hollywood's finest collections of shrunken heads of movie stars and producers.

I thought of Aly Khan and Rubi Rubirosa and the wonderful trophies they had collected during the years.

There was so much to think about and I kept squeezing and squeezing.

All of a sudden, just before I got to Jane Russell, the gun went off. For a second I was blinded but when I looked up the buffalo was gone.

"I got him, I got him!" I shouted.

"The hell you did," said Pierrard. "You missed him by a mile."

"But I hit something. I could hear the thud."

"You hit a Thomas cob antelope which was standing

two hundred yards to the right of the buffalo. Let's have a look."

We crawled up to the animal and found him dead. I had shot him true and straight and he had died brave and strong. I fainted.

The gunbearers and porters whooped for joy.

They threw the antelope on the carrying chair and then they threw me over the antelope and carried the whole mess into camp.

Covello was waiting for us at the camp.

"Where's the buffalo?" he asked.

"I was about to shoot one," I explained, "when I saw this Thomas cob. They're very rare and Pierrard insisted I shoot it instead. What could I do? Buffalo are a dime a dozen, but have you ever seen a Thomas cob like that? He charged me and I had time for only one shot. Fortunately I got him in the chest, right smack in the heart."

Pierrard nodded his head, and gun-bearers didn't speak any English.

The porters gave me the tail of the cob as well as the horns and carried me on their shoulders to the airport in Irumu. It took only a half-day, so I was in my rights when I paid them only ten cents each.

I'm back in Europe now and I can already tell the difference. People are now saying, "Hemingway killed his leopard, Ruark killed his lion and Buchwald killed his Thomas cob."

Now that I'm a full-fledged writer I'm even thinking of writing a book. I've got a great idea for one, about an old man who goes fishing off the coast of Cuba by himself, and catches the biggest fish in the sea only to have the sharks eat it before the old man can get it back to shore. I haven't got a title for it yet, but it should make a whale of a story.

IN DARKEST RUANDA-URUNDI

WHEN ONE VISITS the Belgian Congo, and I believe every self-respecting person should, one must take a trip through Ruanda-Urundi, a small country about the size of Ohio, which is run by the Belgians with the blessings of the United Nations. The Ruanda-Urundi is a rich mandate and a very colourful and beautiful country.

My information on the Ruanda came from an official government guidebook and I was fascinated to read that the Ruanda-Urundi was " . . . a fierce mountainous bastion with great crenellated ramparts, the last refuge of strange men whose physical and psychical contrasts at the same time separate and unite them . . . in the very heart of Africa, a tenacious survival of Biblical times with their shepherd kings and cruel and patriarchal customs . . . a lost world where life continues untroubled to the peaceful voice of nature. . . ."

It sounded pretty good to me, so I flew to Usumbura from Leopoldville and was given a government car to drive for three days through the country. I was also given the names of tribal chiefs, missionaries and functionaries along the way. Naturally I was very interested in meeting a real African chief, no matter how much danger was involved.

I was told that there was a chief at Kayanza, on the road to Astrida, and that it was possible he would talk to me. We were very excited. Israel Shenker, of *Time* and *Life*, and Joe Covello, of *Collier*'s, who were travelling with me, also wanted to meet a native chief, but we were not sure exactly what it would entail.

"If we go to his hut," said Shenker, "don't accept anything to drink. And if he invites us for lunch, say we've got another appointment. We may get poisoned. I hope he dances for us."

I told the other two that I had brought along some crayons from the five-and-ten-cent store which I'd offer as gifts to the chief.

"Maybe he likes cigarettes," Shenker said.

Thus we went forth to meet Chief Baranyanka, ruler of the Watusi tribes between Usumbura and Astrida.

It was easy to find the village and we were given directions to where he lived. While we were busy looking for his hut we passed a large yellow-brick, red-tile-roofed house with a terraced driveway. Eventually someone told us the chief did not live in a hut, but in the yellow-brick house. We rang the doorbell and a tall man in a custom-tailored suit with a striped school tie and Oxford shirt answered the bell.

We asked to speak to the chief and he said in very good French that he was the chief, and invited us into his home. His living room was furnished with modern chairs and a sofa. He had a Stromberg-Carlson radio and gramophone, silver candelabra, modern African sculpture and Persian carpets. Some hut!

"Can I get you something to drink?" he asked us.

Before we could refuse, he gave us our choice of Lanson champagne 1947 or Lanson champagne 1949, Remy Martin cognac, Black and White Scotch and Tuborg beer.

His servant brought out ice cubes and glasses.

Chief Baranyanka explained to us he was a coffee grower and owned plantations over an area of sixty square miles. Since coffee prices had fallen, he hadn't planted a crop this year, but had trimmed his plantations and done some irrigation work.

"How do you get around the country?" I asked him.

"I have a Cadillac and a Buick. I have asthma, so I don't like to fly."

"Do most of the important chiefs have Cadillacs and Buicks?"

"Oh no," he said. "The lesser chiefs—there are twenty-six of us in the Ruanda under the Mwami—have Plymouths, Fords, Chevrolets and Studebakers. Some have only one car."

Baranyanka told us his house had six rooms, but he had another guest house in the back for his children and grandchildren. He was Catholic and attended Mass regularly.

There didn't seem to be much more to say, so, complimenting him on the Lanson 1947, we decided to leave.

Covello whispered, "Maybe he'll invite us to lunch."

But the invitation was not forthcoming.

We got up to leave and shook hands all around. But as we walked toward the car Chief Baranyanka ran after us. "Are these children's crayons yours?"

I said they were and took them from the chief. As we drove away I threw them into the woods right near the chief's new Cadillac.

"A real primitive chief, huh?" Shenker said.

"Sure was," said Covello. "Did you see the fly in his house? And besides, the champagne wasn't really cold enough."

After visiting the chief we decided to see the wild animals in their natural habitat. While some of them have good habitats and others have bad habitats, I believe there is no such thing as a bad animal.

No one who comes to Africa would be caught dead without a camera, and the Congo has one of the happiest photo-hunting grounds in the world. Thousands and thousands of acres of land have been set aside in what is known as Albert National Park, where all animals, regardless of race, creed or colour, are protected by law. It's against the law to kill as much as a mosquito in the park, but the Belgians so far have not imposed any such code on the animals, who are free to do what they want with tourists.

Strangely enough, the animals know they're protected by law and don't seem to begrudge the tourists a picture or two. But they hate to be taken advantage of, and if you hang around too long they might chase you up a tree or down into an anthill. As an experienced African explorer, I've learned a lot about photographing animals in the Albert National Park and perhaps I can pass on some useful information.

Elephants don't mind being photographed at distances of more than thirty feet. Most of them will pose with their families, but when the female has been browbeating the male, then you may be in for trouble. The telltale sign is the elephant raising its ears. This is the time to fold up the camera and go home.

If the elephant is crossing the road in either direction he has the right of way. If he decides to sit in the middle of the road it is up to the automobile to make a detour. Insurance companies are very hard on people who run into elephants, and will not pay for any damage to your fender or the elephant's trunk.

Lions don't mind being photographed at distances of from five to ten feet, providing the cameraman stays in the car and doesn't make any remarks about their manes. But although they will pose for photographers, under no conditions, except extreme hunger, will they roar for tourists. We have been told by game wardens that if you do anything to annoy the male lion the female will attack in a rage. But if you annoy the female, the male will run away. Draw your own conclusions.

Hippopotamuses can usually be found covered up with mud or water, and, unfortunately, if you photograph them in this state they come out in the photos like grey rocks. It's very hard to get a hippo out of water for anything except food. They also like to sit in the middle of the road, and the same traffic rules apply to them as apply to elephants.

Deer and antelope are very courteous to tourists and might even be considered on the hammy side (though they don't taste like ham). They're constantly posing for photographers and using up people's valuable colour film which they should save for the wilder animals.

Wild boar, snakes and crocodiles are camera shy and will snub tourists at the slightest opportunity. But the two animals that have almost a Communist hatred of visiting Americans are the rhino and the buffalo. They go out of their way to be rude to tourists and, unlike the hyena, they have no sense of humour.

There are no special instructions I can give you on photographing rhinos and buffalo. In the case of the latter you might have your camera set at F16 at a 50th of a second, and the buffalo might decide to charge you at 200th of a second, leaving you completely underexposed. This happened recently in the park. A tourist had a buffalo in his sights, and the buffalo had the tourist in his sights. They both focused at the same time and the buffalo charged. This complicated the depth of focus, as the tourist did not want a close-up of the buffalo.

After his friends buried him they developed the tourists' film, and by some good fortune the buffalo was in focus. It was one of the best animal shots ever taken in the Albert National Park.

COWARD IN A JET STREAM

Some time after my victorious return from the Congo, a bemedalled Air Force sergeant came into my office in Paris and said, "Have you ever seen the Eiffel Tower from a jet fighter plane?"

I hemmed and hawed for a while and then cravenly admitted I hadn't.

"Well, we'd like to take you out to Chaumont Air Base and give you a ride."

"What for?"

"We're the 48th Fighter Bomber Wing, otherwise known as the famed Statue of Liberty Wing, and we think we can fly circles around anybody else in Europe. But we haven't had much chance to prove it to civilians. We thought if you took a ride with us we might get our story over to the public."

"Is it dangerous?"

"Of course not. You can fly one of these jets in a wheel-chair. It would be hard to strap you in, but you could do it."

The sergeant was very persuasive, and before I knew what I was doing I said okay.

Saturday was J Day. Two full colonels, three lieutenant-colonels, several majors, captains, and one lieutenant were on hand to greet me. I felt like the chairman of a Congressional Air Force Appropriations Committee.

"IT WAS NICE OF YOU TO COME," one of the colonels shouted as four Sabre Jets flew over our heads.

"WE'VE GOT A NICE LITTLE OLD FLIGHT LINED UP FOR YOU."

"WHAT ARE THOSE JETS DOING UP THERE?" I yelled.

"THEY'RE THE SKY BLAZERS, THE AIR FORCE'S CRACK PRECISION FLYING TEAM. THE FELLOW IN THE LAST PLANE IS JIM REYNOLDS, THE BROTHER OF ALLIE REYNOLDS, THE FORMER NEW YORK YANKEE PITCHER," one of the lieutenant-colonels bellowed proudly.

"THEY'RE PRACTISING FOR A SHOW IN A COUPLE OF WEEKS," a major roared.

"WHEN DO I GET TO SEE THE EIFFEL TOWER?" I cried.

"THERE'S BEEN A CHANGE OF PLANS," one of the colonels shouted. "YOU CAN SEE THE EIFFEL TOWER FROM A JET

ANYTIME, BUT WE THOUGHT SINCE THE SKY BLAZERS WERE
PRACTISING YOU WOULD LIKE TO TAKE A RIDE WITH
THEM."

The noise of the jets drowned out my answer, which
was just as well.

After watching them do some stunts the colonels,
lieutenant-colonels, majors, captains and one lieutenant
took me over to the locker to get me fitted into a G suit.
A G suit looks like a pair of coveralls, but is made in such
a way that your liver won't shoot out of the cockpit when
you come out of a dive. There are pockets all over the G
suit in case you get sick in flight. They gave me a helmet
with an oxygen mask attached. The purpose of the
oxygen mask, it was explained, was to prevent you from
biting your nails in the air. There were sun goggles
attached to the helmet, so when your eyes popped out of
your head there would be a receptacle to catch them.

By this time the Sky Blazers had landed and the four
pilots came into the locker room. I was introduced to
them. The leader of the group was Major William N.
Dillard, of Greenville, South Carolina. He was assisted in
his mad occupation by Captain William Gilmore, of
Dushore, Pennsylvania, First Lieutenant Jack H. Bennett
of Greeley, Colorado, and Captain Jim Reynolds, Allie
Reynold's brother, who, as the lieutenant-colonel pointed
out, had pitched for the New York Yankees.

"Give him a nice easy ride," the colonel said to Major
Dillard as they poked each other in the ribs jokingly.

"You're the first passenger that has ever ridden with the
Sky Blazers," Major Dillard said. "We're as interested in
seeing what happens as you are."

My eyes started bulging and they gave me some oxygen
on the ground. The officers slapped me on the back and
wheeled me out to a two-place jet plane which the Air
Force uses as a training craft to separate the men from
the boys. A sergeant lifted me into the plane and strapped

my legs down tight. Then he strapped my chest, wrapped a parachute around me and fastened the safety belt.

He pointed to a yellow lever just beneath the right side of the seat.

"This will probably never happen, but in case you get into trouble pull that lever and you'll be shot out of the plane, seat and all. Then unfasten your safety belt and pull the rip cord of your parachute."

One of the colonels jumped up on the wings and attached a "hot mike" to our oxygen mask.

"This will probably never happen, but in case you get into trouble pull that lever and you'll be shot out of the plane, seat and all. Then unfasten your safety belt and pull the rip cord."

Major Dillard checked me and said, "This will probably never happen, but . . ."

"ALL RIGHT, ALL READY," I shouted through the oxygen mask.

My plane taxied on to the runway. On my right was Captain William Gilmore's F86 Sabre Jet. On the left was Lieutenant Jack H. Bennett, and in the slot was Captain Jim Reynolds, brother of Allie Reynolds, the former pitcher of the New York Yankees.

The idea seemed to be we were all going to take off at the same time.

Major Dillard's soft South Carolina accent came over the intercom.

"Blazers away."

The four planes roared down the runway. When I opened my eyes I was ten thousand feet over the field.

The nice thing about flying jets is you can't hear the engines. The only noise in the cockpit was the beating of my heart, which had moved up next to the throat mike.

The Sky Blazers, when flying in formation, keep their wing tips about twelve inches from the next plane's. This is to leave enough room between the planes in case a sparrow wants to fly through.

When the team is airborne, the only one who does any talking is Major Dillard.

"Let's try a li'l ole ordinary barrel roll," he said.

A li'l ole ordinary barrel roll, I discovered, is when the pilot rolls the plane in a complete 360-degree spin. The plane comes out of the bottom of the roll at a li'l ole ordinary speed of 420 knots (the reason they call them knots is that that's what happens to your insides).

The first inkling I had that I wasn't flying in a TWA Constellation came when sharp pains started running up my legs. But they didn't stay there long. Suddenly they hit me in the stomach. I had the feeling Rocky Marciano had somehow sneaked into the cockpit and let me have it. At the end of the spin the plane was barrelling along at five hundred miles an hour. I stuck my eyeballs back in their sockets. I looked to see how the other Sabre Jets were doing. They had not moved an inch from our wing tips.

But Major Dillard seemed dissatisfied. "Let's try it again boys, and this time tighten up."

"They looked pretty tight to me, Major," I said.

"I'll give the orders," he replied. "And by the way, if you're going to scream the next time would you please turn off your intercom?"

We did four more barrel rolls before Major Dillard was satisfied. Rocky Marciano was with us on every roll.

"And now," the major said, "a few simple wingovers."

Instead of your eyes popping out of your head, on a wingover they sink back into your brain. Your stomach also contracts, but your legs are numb and you feel no pain. You're sure you'll never pull out of it, but the best thing about it is you don't care. Next we tried a diamond roll, which was followed by a horizontal bomb burst.

When we pulled out of the last one the major asked me, "Did you black out?"

I said I didn't.

"I did," he chuckled.

I started to cry.

The other Blazers had disappeared and Major Dillard said, "There's a beautiful château I want to show you about twenty miles away. We just discovered it the other day. You can't get any idea of the speed of a jet until you fly close to the ground."

With this we dived down to one hundred feet. No one will admit it, but one of the missions of the United States Air Force in France is to keep the hedgerows neat. The American pilots accomplish this by flying at altitudes of from one hundred to ten feet and neatly clipping each hedge as they go by.

We reached the château and flew around it in a circle.

"Did you see it?" he asked me.

"See it? I saw the old countess sitting in the bedroom reading *Bonjour Tristesse* and I don't think the count's going to win that solitaire hand if he doesn't play his black jack on the red queen."

There were no more hedges to cut or châteaux to see, so Major Dillard flew us back to the base.

Willing hands reached up and lifted me out of the cockpit and we all went to the Officers' Club to eat steaks and drink each other's health.

In keeping with the spirit of the day I was placed next to the Sky Blazers, who were seated exactly twelve inches from each other.

I GOT THEIR GOAT

THE BLEVENS DAVIS—Robert Breen production of *Porgy and Bess* had just left Paris for an eleven-week good-will tour of Yugoslavia, Turkey and the Middle East. As an international traveller known for my overflowing good will, I had been asked by the producers to join the troupe when they visited Zagreb, which is sometimes called the Paris of West Yugoslavia, and Belgrade, which is sometimes called the Paris of East Yugoslavia.

Although they couldn't promise me a singing part, they said they would make use of my talents at the first opportunity. It came sooner than anyone expected. The day before the opening, I was asked to scour the environs of Zagreb and hunt down a goat.

Now for those who have never seen *Porgy and Bess*, let me explain that the goat is the most important performer in the show. Just before the final curtain, when Porgy discovers that Bess has left him and gone with Sportin' Life, he says, "Bring my goat," and then he announces he's going north in his goat cart to find Bess. This gives the upbeat to the whole show. As long as Porgy has his goat, there's still a chance he'll find Bess—at least that's the way I've always seen it.

First of all, the one thing the producers thought they wouldn't have any trouble finding in Yugoslavia was a goat. It was assumed that a yoghurt-loving people like the Yugoslavs had more goats than they knew what to do with. But as usual we were proven wrong.

"Goats?" said the hotel manager at the Esplanade. "In Belgrade they got plenty goats, but in Zagreb, population 300,000 peoples, maybe there is 100 goats. You take No. 14 streetcar and get off at Trmje. There maybe you'll find goats."

Before I left, Mr. Walter Riemer, the stage manager, told me exactly what kind of goat he wanted. It had to have horns, and be large enough to pull Porgy across the stage. It couldn't smell, and if it was a female it couldn't be expecting a kid. It had to have a small bag, and its wattles (which hang underneath a goat's chin) had to be the same size. It couldn't have foot-and-mouth disease.

I took along a Yugoslav-French oboe player as an interpreter, and Jimmy Hagerman, assistant stage manager, to
help me carry the goat back to town. Then we grabbed a
No. 14 trolley and went to Trmje.

The first house we went to was owned by a family
named Krnj. The lady admitted she had a goat but said
she was going to kill it that day, as the goat was eating too
much food and wasn't giving enough milk to warrant the
investment. I looked at the goat, but it was too thin and
its wattles were uneven. The lady offered the goat to me for
nothing, but I turned it down. I advised her to kill the goat.

The next house we went to, only two miles from the first
one, was owned by a family named Dnmz. Both their
goats were pregnant and in no mood to go on the stage
of the Zagreb opera house.

The third family, named Fkhg, denied they owned any
goat. They thought we were government men, come to
take their goats away. A recent story in the Zagreb paper
had warned the citizens the government thought there
were too many goats in the city and it was going to do
something about it. The Fkhg family thought we had something to do with confiscating their goats, and they were
going to fight for them. We left without seeing their animals.

Two hours and six miles later we found the house of Mr.
Thlkfbrw. Mr. Thlkfbrw's goat smelled. But he was so
anxious to rent his goat he said, "It is not my goat that
smells—it is me."

Finally we came to the house of Smntch. The Smntchs
owned two goats. One was pregnant and had too much of
a bag, but the other one—I gasped. Her horns were beautiful. Her coat was snowy white. She had no bag at all,
and her beard just made you want to cry. Best of all,
she had the most beautiful wattles I'd ever seen.

I began negotiations on the spot. The goat's name
turned out to be Greta. Mrs. Smntch was not averse to
giving her to *Porgy and Bess* to use, but there were some

thorny questions raised. "Greta," Mrs. Smntch said, through the Yugoslav oboe player, "gives two litres of milk a day. We don't want to give that up."

I agreed to let Mrs. Smntch come to the opera house twice a day to milk Greta.

Then there was the question of food. Greta likes only hay from the Smntch farm.

I agreed to feed her only Smntch hay.

How much would I pay for Greta?

We made a package deal. In exchange for Greta and the Smntch's fourteen-year-old son to take care of her, I would pay one thousand dinars (three dollars) a day. All milk from the party of the first part (which would be allowed to be milked twice daily) would go to the Smntch family, and the hay that the party of the first part did not eat would become the property of the Smntchs to do with what they wished.

The contract was signed. Then, since we couldn't get Greta on the streetcar, we had to walk to the theatre. This made her slightly irritable, and the company had to buy twelve cubes of sugar before she agreed to go on.

Needless to say, Greta was the hit of the show. She was the only Yugoslav performer on the stage that night and the audience gave her a rousing ovation. The evening Greta Smntch went on at the opera house will long be remembered as the night a new star was born.

CRASHING THE *SAUNA* BARRIER

IT NEVER OCCURRED to me to go to Finland. Not that I had anything against Finland personally; it was just that, with Paavo Nurmi retired, there didn't seem much reason for going there. But a nice man from Finnair, the nationalized Finnish airlines, told me that they were opening a new route from Paris to Helsinki and offered me a free ride to celebrate the occasion. They even said they'd treat me to a Finnish bath and throw in a reindeer-steak dinner. With these choice morsels dangled in front of my eyes, I had no reason to refuse, and I can't say I'm sorry.

The one word that constantly crops up in everybody's conversation in Finland is *sauna*—the native Finnish bath. But in Finland a sauna is not just a bath—it is a way of life. A sauna is to a Finn what a pub is to a Britisher, what a café is to a Frenchman, what a television set is to an American. The whole social life of the family revolves around the sauna. People build their saunas before they build their houses. Business deals, marriages, divorces and even births are transacted in a sauna. The world trembles, governments topple, fortunes fall, but the Finnish bath has remained the same ever since the prehistoric day when an anonymous Slav (or was it a Teuton?) poured some cold water on some hot rocks and started to perspire.

"What a wonderful idea," he was quoted as telling a *Time* correspondent. "This is better than taking a bath. I predict a great future for saunas."

Little did he know how right he would be.

The typical Finnish sauna is a single-room log building with stones on top of an uncovered furnace. When the sauna is heated the smoke is not let out but allowed to circulate around the room, heating the ceiling, the walls and the benches. Hence, if a man sits in such a room for any length of time he must produce either blood, sweat or tears.

Every hotel in Finland has a sauna, and there is nothing more pleasing for a foreigner than to tell the room clerk to prepare one for him at the end of a hard sightseeing day. Usually, if you time it right, a sauna can take the place of the cocktail hour, and the price, I'm happy to add, is no higher than the price of a dry martini.

I had extraordinary luck the day I decided to take one at the Hotel Vakunna in Helsinki. I was given for an attendant the very same woman who had given a sauna to movie actor Gregory Peck when he paid a visit to Helsinki last year. Her name was Leena, and when it was revealed in the newspapers that she had given Peck a Finnish bath, she became the most sought-after sauna attendant in all of Finland. Next to meeting Jan Sibelius there is no greater honour in Finland than to be given a bath by Leena of the Vakunna.

Leena, a strapping, husky woman in her fifties, is a modest rubber, and to look at her you would never think she had met Gregory Peck, much less given him a sauna. But next to her heart of gold is nothing but tough muscle, and when you're put in Leena's hands, bones crack, legs go limp and heads go spinning on the floor.

Leena made me strip completely and then, with a gentle shove, threw me into the torture chamber. She grabbed a pail of cold water and threw it on red-hot rocks. Steam started to rise in the room. The second pail of cold water she threw on the corpse writhing on the floor.

Then she threw more water on the rocks. The temperature of the room had reached the melting point of steel, but Leena did not seem satisfied. Suddenly I realized what she was trying to do. She was trying to crash the sauna barrier. I yelled through the mist, "Please don't make it any hotter than you made it for Gregory Peck."

She didn't seem to hear me.

Finally she stuck a long cake tester in me and realized I was done.

Then Leena took a bundle of birch branches and started whipping the body. The Finns will tell you they do this to give your corpse a nice fragrance, but actually it's so the victim can't smell his own burning flesh. Leena whisked me from the top down, and in no time at all she was whisking the soles of my feet.

"It's very important that the soles of the feet should be well whisked," she explained. "Only a well-whisked man knows the true glories of a sauna. Even Gregory Peck looked better after he was whisked."

After the whisking I was given a bath and then rinsed off with water. The Finns prefer to jump in a lake or roll in the snow after their sauna but since the Vakunna sauna is located on the seventh floor of a building and there was no snow in Helsinki at that time of year, Leena let me off lightly with a 31-degree-Fahrenheit shower. She then wrapped me in one of the hotel's towels and let me thaw out in a quiet hospital bed in a little room off the bath.

I've had other saunas while I've been in Finland, even one above the Arctic Circle in Lapland, but as far as I'm concerned the one Leena gave me at the Vakunna was the highlight of my trip. I can't help believing in some small way that a little of Gregory Peck has rubbed off on me.

ALONE IN NO MAN'S LAPLAND

"AND NOW THAT you've seen Helsinki," the man from the Finnish Tourist Office said, "how would you like to visit Lapland?"

"Why?" I inquired.

"Because," he said, "you will see nothing like it anywhere. For the first time you will come to real grips with the mysterious forces of the North. You will see vast trackless wilds of virgin forests and naked hills, strapping

B

spruces, sunny summits, bristling birches, earthy bots, matted moss, stilted cranes, frosty forests, boggy bilberries, fertile fields, whining willows, turbulent tundra, ranting reindeer, lonely Laplanders, lusty logrollers, wily wolves, fidgety foxes, bumbling bears, countless caves, piny paradises, raging rivers, shining streams, windy wastelands, dazzling dam sites, haughty herdsmen, doughty dogs, salty salmon, harried herrings, carefree cattle, steaming saunas, fearless fodder, mushy marshlands, towering timber, swollen swamps, fragrant firs, fetching fountainheads, mucky mire, misty meadows, stunted sycamores and muted minks."

"How many marks for the dollar?" I inquired.

"Three hundred and forty to the dollar," my man said.

"Good. I'll go."

For the trip I bought burly boots, woolly vests and frantic fur caps. I also bought twenty-four dollars' worth of beads in case I met any Laplanders.

As the DC3 rose high above the town towers of Helsinki I took my last look at civilization as we westerners know it. For the next three days I would come to grips with the mysterious forces of the North. I knew for the first time how Perry, Byrd, Cook and Nanook must have felt when they took off for the frozen wastelands. I could see the National Geographic Society awarding me a medal; the Explorers Club would probably give me an honorary membership.

The plane landed first at Oulu, then at Kemi, and finally, as the cold Arctic wind blew across the cold Arctic night, the plane landed unceremoniously at Rovaniemi, the capital of Finnish Lapland. As the airport bus made its way along the dark road the first thing I saw in primitive Lapland was a modern Esso gasoline station. The second thing I saw was a brilliantly lighted hotel which had a large lobby, a bath in every room and a six-piece orchestra in the restaurant playing the "Song from Moulin Rouge."

"Where are the reindeer and Laplanders?" I inquired of the maître d'hôtel.

"Ah," he said regretfully, "you must go north."

The next morning I took out my compass and hailed a bus going north, north to Ivalo, north to the Arctic Sea. Widespread they stand, the Northland's dusky forests.

I stopped at Sodankylä, far above the Arctic Circle, thirsting for some reindeer milk and some Lapland small talk. But instead I found a modern Esso gasoline station and three general stores all running sales of Kellogg's Corn Flakes, Lux Flakes and chlorophyll toothpaste.

"Where are the reindeer and Laplanders?" I inquired of a traffic policeman.

"North," he said.

The bus started north. I saw forests and lakes, lakes and forests, and finally, as the bus kept wending its way, I saw snow. First there was a blotch here; then a blotch there and at last the whole woods were blanketed with a white carpet.

At last I reached Ivalo, which, according to the map, was a tiny outpost in an uncharted wilderness. There were no Esso stations. All there was was a Gulf gas station. The three general stores had corn flakes, Lux Flakes and chlorophyll toothpaste, and it was so primitive they were featuring one-cent sales.

"Where are the reindeer and Laplanders?" I asked Mrs. Helstorm, manager of the Ivalo Hotel.

"You must go north," she told me.

The next day I went to Lake Inari, where I found a man fishing in a hole in the ice. He had never seen a reindeer, but his grandfather had, somewhere, he said, up north. He advised me to speak to a man in the tiny village of Inari who spoke English and might know the whereabouts of a reindeer herd.

I sought him out, this man who might know about reindeer. His name was Enok Kangasniemi and he had served in the First World War as an American soldier. Now he lived near the roof of the world, fishing, hunting and building, enjoying the long sleep of the Arctic winter and the golden fruits of the midnight sun.

Yes, Enok himself had seen reindeer. He even knew Laplanders who owned herds. But unfortunately both herds and Laplanders were out in the forests now. There was one Laplander named Aikiv who owned two thousand head, more even than his brother, who had possibly fifteen hundred, and if I went further up perhaps I would find them.

But Enok said the Aikiv brothers might come into Inari with their reindeer in the springtime, and if I wanted to wait I could kill two birds with one stone. I thanked him for his advice, but told him that I was afraid that a man who waits in the Arctic is lost. I had to move on, north, of course.

Enok seemed sad that he couldn't help me. "Perhaps," he said, "you would like to see a cave where a bear once hibernated."

I postponed my departure and Enok took me out into the forests, out into Suomi's land, out past the wondrous Lake Inari, billowing and driving the blue waters against the lumbering logs and crackling kindling, far out into the virgin backlands of no man's land. There we climbed a hill, pressing forward, ignoring the tragic spell that Mother Nature had wrought on her most northern children.

And finally we found it, the very cave where once a bear had laid his weary bones to rest, to sleep through the bleak long night, warm and unafraid, for sleep is the only protection the Arctic bear knows against the timeless darkness. I crawled into the cave on my hands and knees, perhaps in the very same manner that the bear had many long winters ago. O primitive North, what mysteries are hidden in your silent caverns?

Then Enok lit a match and I looked around the walls of the cave, expecting to see a mural from some prehistoric tribe. There were many inscriptions on the walls. I read one. It said: "Sam Schoomaker and Harry Bloom, of the University of Michigan, visited this cave July 7, 1951."

Further down were listed the names of seven women on a Cook's Tour from Jacksonville, Florida, and across on another cave wall the simple inscription "John—Helen" was framed in a heart with an arrow running down the centre.

"Enough of this wild Lapland life," I told Enok. "I must go north if I ever expect to find reindeer and Laplanders."

My compass wavered slightly. It had never been this far north before. Before long I saw the fells of Norway off in the distance. The Arctic Sea was dead ahead, and not much farther away the North Pole. But where, oh where, were the galloping reindeer and the gentle Laplanders? In Utjokki I laid my problem, through an interpreter, before the wise man of the village.

I had come, I told him, from a far-off land, in search of reindeer and Laplanders.

"At the moment there are no reindeer around here," he said. "The Laplanders have taken them in the forests to graze."

"North?" I inquired.

"No, not north, south."

"South! Where's that?"

"Just follow the road you came up on. You'll find it. And would you do me a favour, if you pass through Ivalo? Would you ask the lady in the general store to send me up by the next bus a box of Kellogg's Corn Flakes and six tubes of chlorophyll toothpaste?"

A NEW LEASE ON TEXAS

ALTHOUGH A Yankee by birth, I've always had a warm spot in my heart for Texas, and if people think I plan to make fun of this here fine state or the patriotic people in it they're plumb out of their minds. I'm pro-Texas and I'm plumb sick and tired of Yankees and foreigners making light of it.

In order to show how fond of Texas I am, I went up to Gainesville recently and bought me an oil lease. If there is anything that separates a Texan from other people it's an oil lease. It don't matter what part of the state you got your lease in, as long as there's oil in the ground you're as a good a Texan as the next fellow.

I was fortunate when looking for my lease to have with me Jefferson S. Ewing, general superintendent of one of the largest independent oil companies in the Southwest. Jeff, who has been drilling for oil for over thirty-five years, tried to discourage me in my project. "You only hit one out of eight if you're lucky. You'd have a better chance shooting craps."

I laughed. "What if Sid Murchison, or Clint Richardson, or Bob Hope had thought that way? Where would they be now? Jeff, I know there's oil in Texas and we're going to find it."

Jeff shrugged his shoulders and flew me up to Gainesville in a private plane to see if we could pick me up a lease. The most important man in Gainesville is a fellow named Fred Snuggs, who is a lease broker. Fred is a fellow who contacts farmers and gets them to sell their mineral rights to oil operators like myself. We compensate the farmer for the lease and when we hit oil we give him an eighth of the profits in royalties. There's nothing wrong with that.

Mr. Snuggs took us to his office in the Turner Hotel.

"I got a few leases," he said. "Do you want a producing or a nonproducing land lease?"

"Nonproducing, of course," I told him. "Why take the gambling fun out of it?"

"Well, I got a nice forty-acre lease that runs until November. It's known as the Horne Lease out of the T. P. Henry Survey. It's located between the Walnut Bend and Callisburg fields. Someone brought in a well just a mile and a quarter south-east of it recently and they say it runs right toward the Horne property."

Mr. Snuggs showed me a map with the Horne Lease clearly marked. "Of course, I better warn you there are drawbacks to it. For one thing the noise from the pumping of the wells all around it will keep you awake at night. And for another there's so much oil around that part of the country that the water's hardly fit to drink. And for a third, if the major oil companies find out you bought the Horne Lease they'll bother the daylights out of you to buy it away."

My mouth was watering. "I'll take it. How much?"

"Ten dollars," said Mr. Snuggs. "But you have to pay any damages to the farm when the well comes in."

Jeff said I made a good deal. "Now you have to start some rumours around to make your property worth something."

We went into the Turner Hotel coffee shop for lunch.

Mr. Snuggs introduced me to a Mr. Hurley, the Cadillac dealer in Gainesville. We shook hands warmly. "I just bought the Horne Lease, Mr. Hurley," I said in a loud whisper, "and I'll probably be in to see you in the next few days."

"You're doing fine," Jeff told me.

Miss Zella Allen, who has a radio programme in Gainesville, wanted to know what I was doing in town.

"If you promise not to tell anyone, I'll let you know."

Miss Allen promised.

"I was in the Ritz Bar in Paris and this fellow at the next table mentioned something about the Horne Lease in Gainesville and I decided to hop over and get it before he did. But for heaven's sake don't say anything about it. If the major companies find out I've bought the H-O-R-N-E Lease they'll drive me crazy. I cherish privacy."

Miss Allen rushed out of the restaurant.

Jeff said, "I'm proud of you."

I tried one more ploy. "GET MR. H. L. HUNT ON THE PHONE!" I shouted to the waitress.

When the waitress got Mr. Hunt's office I took the phone.

"H. L., I GOT A PROBLEM. I BOUGHT IN THE HORNE LEASE AND HAVEN'T HAD TIME TO DRILL YET. BUT THE TENANT FARMER ON THE LAND SAYS IF I DON'T DRAIN OFF THE OIL SO HIS CATTLE STOP SLIPPING ON THE GRASS HE'S GOING TO COMPLAIN TO THE A.S.P.C.A."

The dining room emptied out in thirty seconds.

"I guess there's nothing for you to do now," said Jeff, "but go back to Dallas and see about joining the Petroleum Club."

But the first thing an oil operator does when he strikes it rich in Texas is head for Neiman-Marcus, the most elegant store, Texans believe, in the entire United States of America.

Neiman-Marcus makes it easy on oil people. They'll assign one man to you personally to take you through the entire store and help you make your purchases.

I was given Dudley Ramsden, the head of the jewellery department. I explained to him I had simple tastes and didn't want anything ostentatious, no matter what it cost me.

The first thing I bought was a six-and-a-half-gallon hat.

The ten-gallon hat went out in Texas with the ten-gallon bottle of wine, and you can carry almost any bottle in a six-and-a-half-gallon hat now.

"What else do I need?"

Mr. Ramsden suggested a vicuña Eisenhower battle jacket.

"It's only $225, and every oilman should have at least one," he said.

I bought two.

"You've got some uranium cuff links, haven't you?"

I said no.

Mr. Ramsden found this unbelievable. "Then come with me."

He took me to the cuff-link counter and put a pair on me. Then he produced a Geiger counter. "You see," he said, "it registers ·4 and it's still safe for humans to wear."

"How much is it?"

"It's $38·50 for the cuff links, and only $195 for the Geiger counter."

I bought a half dozen of each.

Mr. Ramsden had me fitted for a $600 vicuña suit, a $50 pair of alligator shoes and a dozen $20 gold ties.

"And now I'd like something purty for the little woman."

He took me up to the lingerie department and showed me an $1,850 mink-trimmed housecoat-and-pyjama set, which I immediately bought, and a solid lace slip for $150.

I also bought a $550 do-it-yourself diamond-cutting tool set, a $50 mink stole for my three-year-old niece, and a $75 pair of cashmere blue jeans for my two-and-one-half-year-old son.

After Neiman-Marcus I went to see Margaret Sedwick, Texas's leading interior decorator. I told Miss Sedwick I wanted a simple ranch house overlooking my oil wells.

She suggested a rambling two-story thirty-room ranch building with the landing strip on the side of the house instead of at the back. The hangars would be done in native stone and the stables in California redwood.

She said she would provide all the stuffed animals for the trophy room but I'd have to find the record sailfish on the open market.

"Would you like some oil paintings?"

"Of course," I replied. "I'm in the oil business, aren't I? Let's have a half-dozen crude oil paintings."

Then I explained to her that I didn't want to spoil my son, but I did want him to be happy.

Miss Sedwick said, "I understand. We'll build a little play yard for him which he can walk out to from his bedroom. The palomino-pony stables will be in easy reach and we'll build a miniature oil well with oil gushing out of it on his sand pile."

"It's good as far as it goes," I said, "but, Miss Sedwick, I love that kid."

"Well," she said, "why don't we install a closed television circuit for him? We could build a studio a half mile away from the house and fly down Howdy Doody, Kukla, Fran and Ollie, Pinky Lee and Walt Disney to put on shows for him. It will be the only closed child's TV circuit in Texas."

I could have kissed her for the idea.

"The last thing I want," I said, "is something different in a swimming pool."

"I have just the thing for you," she replied. "A friend of mine has just designed a new swimming pool in the shape of Liberace."

I said I'd take it.

"With or without the candelabra in the centre?" she asked.

"With," I said. "How else could I swim at night?"

After going to Neiman-Marcus and buying a home, the only thing I had to do was join a petroleum club. The

Dallas Petroleum Club is probably one of the most exclusive ones in the country, limited to 500 resident members and 550 non-resident members. With all the gas and oil being discovered in Texas these days you can imagine what kind of waiting list the club has.

One of the rules of the club is that 90 per cent of the man's income must come from oil before he is admitted. This apparently was the only thing holding up my membership. But I still wanted to show I had the right spirit and the will to be a member.

I wandered up to a group of men at the luncheon table and said, "Howdy, fellows. Do any of you have ten hundred-dollar bills for a thousand-dollar bill? I want to light my cigar."

There was an awkward silence, so I lit my cigar with the thousand-dollar bill instead. They realized I was one of them and they relaxed and continued talking.

"Eisenhower had no right to veto that gas bill," one of the men said.

"You're darn right he didn't," I concurred.

"We get eleven cents a thousand feet and the gas companies back East get two fifty a thousand," another man said.

"I'd just as soon let the stuff blow into the air as pipe it out at that price," a third producer announced.

"And do you know who will suffer by it?" the man on my right asked.

"THE PEOPLE ARE GOING TO SUFFER—THAT'S WHO," I shouted.

"You're darn right. If we can't sell our gas under the free-enterprise system the way the Almighty intended it to be sold then we might as well not sell it at all."

"What are we sitting here for?" I asked excitedly. "Let's go to Washington and give them a piece of our mind."

"We must not be hasty," someone replied. "Don't forget

they could still give us trouble on the depreciation-tax bill."

"But we earned the bill," I protested. "Not one of us would drill for oil if we had no depreciation allowances. Don't forget a can of oil isn't like a can of beans. You can always replace a can of beans on the grocer's shelf, but once you take oil out of the ground, you can't put it back again."

They all shook hands with me to congratulate me on the way I put it.

"They even want a bite out of you when you die," another man said.

"Those inheritance taxes just kill you," the man on my left added. "I don't care for myself, but what about my kids?"

"What about all our kids?" I said, hitting the table with my fist. "Every day the government throws our money down the sewer that should go in our wee ones' bank accounts."

The men listened with rapt attention.

"There is only one thing to do," I said. "We've got to get into our private planes and fly on to Washington. Once they see the whites of our eyes they'll think twice about vetoing gas bills and passing inheritance taxes. Are we going to let this country be eaten up by government bureaucrats, or are we going to face the challenge as Custer did at the Alamo?"

There was a strained silence and finally one of the men said, "Custer wasn't at the Alamo."

I tried to cover up. "Well, if he had been maybe we would have won."

"Where did you say you were from, stranger?" one of the men asked suspiciously.

"Paris," I replied.

"Paris, Texas?"

"Paris, France," I weakly replied.

"I knew it," said the man on my right. "A foreigner."

"But," I protested, "I'm one of you. I own the Horne Lease in Gainesville. Honest, I'm as much against this gas veto as any man in this room. I'm a lobbyist at heart."

They would not believe me, and two of the larger men saw me to the door, making sure my feet did not touch the rug on the way out.

"Custer, my foot," one of them said, and he kicked me for a field goal.

MY CONQUEST OF THE EMPIRE STATE

I READ IN A New York paper some time ago that Sir Edmund Hillary, conqueror of Mount Everest, was visiting Manhattan and had made an ascent of the formidable Empire State Building. It suddenly occurred to me that if Sir Edmund could climb the Empire State Building, so could I.

Why do men want to climb buildings? No one can really say. Perhaps the great danger attracts them—the terrible uncertainty about what is waiting for them at the next floor, the unquenched desire to attempt the possible for its own sake, the comradeship and the sense of achievement that come from doing something the easy way. Once you've reached the top of a building you'll never want to live on the ground floor again.

And so it was with me. The Empire State Building is a forbidding monument of rock and granite, its bold, bare face staring out over a sea of lesser and uglier buildings and only partly air-conditioned. The Empire State Building had to be conquered or I would die in the attempt.

Since I knew the problem would not be easy I hired a Sherpa porter named Jay Tensing Scott from the Ben

Sonnenberg public-relations office. The Sonnenberg office has the Empire State for an account and their porters know it better than anybody else.

Scott advised me that I had to prepare for the trip. Fortunately I could purchase supplies on the ground floor. I bought food from Longchamps, chlorophyll toothpaste from the Walgreen drugstore, nightgowns from Wallachs and money from the Manufacturers Trust Company.

On February 5 at exactly ten sixteen a.m. we started to make the ascent. Scott advised me to do it by stages, so the first thing we did was take the local elevator to the sixth floor and set up our first camp. We were both very fresh and we made it quite easily. But as we got off we ran into our first difficulty. There was a sign in the hall, USE NIGHT ELEVATORS AFTER 7 P.M. AND ON SATURDAYS AND SUNDAYS. Suppose, I thought to myself, shuddering, we didn't get down by 7 p.m. . . . but I didn't think about it long.

Since we were making such good time we decided to keep going as long as we could. We took the elevator to the twenty-seventh floor and made our second camp. It was right in front of the Arlene Dahl lingerie and night-gown company, and although I intended to camp there for three days Scott urged me to go on.

We passed up the thirty-third floor, where the Iron and Steel Institute was, in favour of a much better camping site on the thirty-fifth floor, where the Schenley whisky company maintains its offices. It was a smart decision, as it gave me a chance to refurbish our supplies. By this time we were both breathing pretty heavily and my loyal Sherpa porter suggested we stop at the Jantzen bathing-suit offices on the fifty-first floor and catch our breath.

We stayed there for several minutes catching our breath and losing it again. Scott, the plucky little fellow, insisted we keep going up. We both put on oxygen masks and started up again. Up past the First National Bank of

Boston, up past the Brookhaven Atomic Bomb Project, higher than I. Miller shoes and the Innocenti Italian motor-scooter company.

But we didn't dare stop. At the eightieth floor we zoomed past the New York Knickerbocker basketball team and at the eighty-second floor the Animal Welfare Institute, and finally past the WOR-TV studio on the eighty-third. Before I knew it we were on the eighty-sixth floor, where we set up the last camp before trying to reach the summit.

It was primitive but satisfactory. There were ladies' and men's washrooms, a snack bar, a water fountain, phone booths and a recording studio where you could make records and send them to friends in other parts of the world. I started to feel a sense of power, a sense of exhilaration, a sense of loneliness. Only fifteen million people had visited the eighty-sixth floor before us. For the first time in our lives we were alone.

But we hadn't got to the top yet. It was now eleven fifteen. We scrambled on the elevator, avoiding too-severe-looking cornices, and rose slowly and carefully to the hundred and second floor. My faculties started to get numb.

From here on we had to climb. Scott belayed me and I belayed Scott. We climbed past a door marked FOR EMPLOYEES ONLY, then up a ladder with a sign, PRO-TECTED BY THE WM. J. BURNS AGENCY, and still up past NO SMOKING warnings, until at last we opened a trap door and stood on the hundred and fifth floor.

We had reached the summit. As we both hung on to the WJZ television aerials we embraced each other. The moment that the whole world had waited for was upon us. We tied a United Nations flag to an NBC-TV aerial and an American flag to a CBS pipeline, and then, after taking photographs as the cruel wind beat around our faces, we made the difficult descent by an express elevator straight down to the ground.

In years to come there will be arguments and debates

as to who got to the top of the Empire State Building first.
Scott will claim he did, but the truth is I got there ahead
of him. You can't believe a word these Sherpa porters
tell you.

FLYING WITH CHILD

TRAVELLING IS a pleasure instead of an ordeal when
you go by air with baby or junior. It is wise to notify your
airline ahead of time, however, so they will have certain
things aboard for baby's comfort. . . .

If he is a little older, make a game out of acquainting
him with the objects around him. By the time he leaves
the ground he will feel quite at home. You might take
along a favourite toy to keep him busy and add to his
feeling of security.

Children love to fly. They enjoy the excitement of
boarding the big plane and watching the clouds go by the
window. It is an experience they'll remember always and
cherish. And so will Mother, because of the time and
effort it has saved her in travelling with small fry.

From a pamphlet distributed
by the Air Transport Association

I was reading this pamphlet on a flight across the
Atlantic Ocean recently. Standing next to me on the seat,
reading over my shoulder, was a two-and-one-half-year-
old boy who happens to be related to me.

There are certain things I would like to call to the attention of the Air Transport Association at this time. I followed their instructions to a T and it's apparent that the
person who wrote the pamphlet has never flown higher
than a thirty-inch desk.

In the first place, it's not as easy to take along a child's favourite toy as the article would imply. In my case X Jr.'s favourite toy happened to be a three-and-one-half-foot red-and-yellow stuffed Teddy bear. Although Pan American wanted my child to feel secure they pointed out that all stuffed Teddy bears three feet or over took up as much space as a two-and-one-half-year-old child and were subject to the same fare. We had to leave the bear at home. As soon as he boarded the plane, X Jr.'s insecurity was apparent.

He refused to buckle his safety belt and tripped the stewardess as she was explaining how to use a life jacket properly. As an afterthought he howled through the whole demonstration and I'm quite sure that if the emergency ever arose there were very few people on the plane who would know what to do.

Once the plane was safely in the air and out of danger, X Jr. decided to fasten his seat belt. It took his mother and his father and a stewardess to get it unfastened.

Children are usually fed first on a plane. In theory this is a good idea, but in practice it works like this. The child, having finished *his* meal and noticing other passengers are just starting theirs, will wander down the aisle staring at the people while they eat. Few people can stare down a child, and before I got wind of what was happening X Jr. had managed to procure three pieces of cake, a lamb chop and a cup of salad dressing.

Following the article's suggestion, I made a game out of acquainting X Jr. with objects around him. If he pushed the light switch he got one point. If he pushed the buzzer for the stewardess he got three points. If he pulled out the ash tray he got five points, and if he hit the person in front of him he got fifteen points. When he received a total of fifty points, he got the spanking of his life.

When a child gets bored with "watching the clouds go by the window" (it usually takes about thirty seconds), he will head for the water fountain. The water fountain to a child is by far the most interesting part of an aeroplane. Aeronautical engineers, realizing this, have designed the fountains so that the water buttons are out of reach of tiny hands. Few children are daunted by this measure. In X Jr.'s case he stole a woman's jewellery case and someone else's movie camera and a copy of *Andersonville*. By piling them up he not only managed to reach the water button, but was also successful in destroying a month's supply of Pan American's paper cups.

The question of whether a parent should let his child wander up and down the aisle during the night or keep him in his seat is something each person must work out in his own conscience.

If you let the child wander you can probably get some sleep—but nobody else on the plane can. At three o'clock in the morning X Jr. was serving Life Savers and chewing gum to the other passengers, or so I was told the next morning by several blood-shot people.

There is no doubt that travelling with a child is a memorable experience that everyone would like to forget.

Lindbergh had the right idea. He flew the Atlantic alone.

WEEK-END WITH THE MOB

ONE DAY IN Paris after I had become a recognized authority on the European underworld I interviewed an Italian deportee named Frank Frigenti, a convicted murderer who claimed that he had been on intimate terms with Al Capone, had knowledge of many crimes committed by deportees, and who said that he had once organized a march of deportees in Rome which never came off.

You can imagine my surprise when I received word from Naples shortly afterwards that Mr. Frigenti had told me some untruths. These letters from other deportees said some horrible things about Mr. Frigenti. For one thing, they said that Mr. Frigenti had never met Al Capone and that the only thing he knew about him was what he had read in the newspapers. For another, they said Mr. Frigenti's knowledge of crime was culled from detective magazines.

"We chased him out of Naples," one correspondent wrote, "after he came out of the hospital for twenty-six days. One of the boys gave him a kicking around because he squealed on somebody. He receives his stories from police magazines and then sells them. He is a writer like I am, and I'm no writer. His stories have made our future very detrimental; if you do not believe what I am telling you, I am willing to tell it to you in front of that punk Frank Frigenti.

"We would like to invite you down to Naples as our guest and see how us deportees are getting along; you would get astonishing stories of our conditions here. Best wishes to you from all deportees."

Well, it's hard to turn down an invitation like that, so I went down to Naples to see if all the untruths Frank Frigenti told me were untrue.

I arrived on a Saturday morning and was met by a delegation of two deportees (the Naples police frown on delegations of more than two or three deportees for any occasion). One introduced himself as Nick Di Marzo, who had done time for narcotics, counterfeiting and ship jumping. Mr. Di Marzo's last Stateside address was Lewisburg Federal Pen, where, as the prison barber, he cut the hair on the heads of such famous men as Frank Costello, Harry Gold, Alger Hiss and David Greenglass. My other escort was Enofrio Raimondo, who had a white-slavery rap in his past and was asked to leave the country for embezzling $25,000 from some liquor people.

Both men apologized for their appearance, but explained that they were short on good clothes. I told them to forget it.

"What was the last time you saw Frigenti?" Mr. Di Marzo asked.

"About two weeks ago. Why do you ask?"

"If that bum ever comes back to Naples the boys are waiting for him. How can he say we're in dope and girls? Why, we'd be rich if this were the truth."

"We have prepared an intinerary for you," said Mr. Raimondo. "We're going to show you everything you want to see. You can ask any questions you want to ask; our life is an open book."

"That bum Frank Frigenti!" Mr. Di Marzo said. "Where does he come off calling himself a big-time gangster? He's a bum."

"But he did kill his mother-in-law, didn't he?" I asked.

"Probably—but if he did, it was a crime of passion."

Mr. Raimondo told me that there were about one hundred deportees in Naples, many of whom did not belong there. Only a few, like Mike Spinelli and Lucky Luciano, had any money when they came. The rest were loaded on to ships and planes and arrived with very little in the way of spending money. When a man is deported from the United States to Italy he is greeted at the boat by the Italian police, who escort him to his place of birth.

"For most of us," said Mr. Di Marzo, "our place of birth is on the top of a mountain somewhere, with maybe two donkeys and one goat in the town. How are we going to live there?"

At his place of birth, the deportee registers and is given an identity card. Deportees must remain in the town where they were born, but most of them head for the port cities of Genoa, Naples and Palermo, where it is easier to make a living.

"The word deportee is a black mark," said Mr. Raimondo. "The Italians don't want us, the Americans don't want us. To Americans we're Italians and to the Italians we're Americans. We advocate democracy more than anyone else, but do you call this democracy? Italy is the country that God forgot to bless."

"Lots of these guys," said Mr. Di Marzo, "can't even speak Italian. They were taken to America as kids in their mothers' arms. Most of us would rather be in prison in the United States than free men here. I got two years at Lewisburg because I asked for it. I told the judge that I would rather be there than for them to send me out of the country."

"We're always defending America to the Italians," Mr. Raimondo said. "These people say that American cars are no good, American food stinks. These people got us Americans down as bums and that gets us deportees sore. We fight them many times. They really can't be blamed. They have never seen America."

"You know something?" said Mr. Di Marzo. "I am more American than you are. I even went to school on the GI Bill of Rights, in Rome. I got an honourable discharge from the Army. What am I doing in Italy?"

Mr. Raimondo said, "Let's go see some of the boys."

I took one last look at the Bay of Naples, gulped, and followed them down through some narrow alleys to a dark bay street near the Naples port.

"The reason we come to Naples," said Mr. Raimondo, "is because it's the only place we can hustle. It's a port. There are ships coming in all the time, and merchant-marine guys befriend us. We'd go crazy if it wasn't for the port."

He explained that most of the deportees arriving from

the United States were flat broke and unable to get legitimate work in Naples. The only thing they could do was wait for American ships to come into port and to offer to escort sailors and passengers around the city. As a man needed a licence for this kind of work, the Italians would tip off the police, and the police would usually clamp down hard on them.

We ended up in a small, dingy restaurant near the port. There were six or seven deportees sitting around, and four or five drifted in while we were talking. I was introduced to a man called "Joe the Wop" (narcotics), "Little Joe" (narcotics), "Blackie Joe" (armed robbery), "Dominici" (robbery), "Pop" (robbery) and "Mickey" (attempted murder), and so on. Most of them told me that they had been framed and weren't doing anything more than getting caught in a crap game or playing the horses away from the tracks.

They were all interested in knowing how Frank Frigenti's health was. Mr. Frigenti had sold some stories on deportees which apparently gave a dark picture of their situation, and they resented it. They resented it so much that they asked me to tell Mr. Frigenti that if he ever cared to visit Naples again he would receive a welcome heretofore unheard of in the annals of the American underworld.

"He's a disgrace to deportees," the man named Pop said. "I'm fifty-one years old, but I can't wait to get my hands on him. He said we dealt in dope and girls. It's a big lie."

"Let's be frank," said Mr. Di Marzo. "We couldn't get into any of the rackets if we wanted to. Look at it this way: the Italian government's got the numbers racket with the national lottery. You can place a bet anywhere you want in Italy, so there is no illegal bookmaking. There are no card games and no crap games. If we try to get into contraband, the Italian contrabandists finger us and we're hauled off to jail. You can't sell junk [dope] in Naples. If we tried to heist [stick up] a bank, everybody would start yelling at once. These people in Naples don't mind their own business. And they ain't afraid of guns. You show them a gun, they'll spit in your eye. Besides, you can't make a getaway. Where could you go? It's these identification papers, they drive us nuts. Every time something happens, they start screaming at the deportees. As far as we're concerned, the United States dropped the bomb on the wrong country."

"Do these men," said Joe the Wop, "look like they could shoot anybody? They ain't even got the strength to hold a gun in their hands."

"Sure," said Pop, "we've made mistakes. But even a baby has to tumble before he walks. If they're willing to accept nine out of ten refugees—you can't tell me they ain't Communists—then why they keeping us good Americans out?"

Blackie Joe said his son was an American soldier. "If my son's good enough to be an American soldier, why should they take his father away from his family?"

"Suppose," said a man named Willie, "Italy goes to war against the United States. Then Blackie Joe's son will have to shoot his father. Is that justice?"

"Italy's the only one accepting deportees," said Mr. Raimondo. "Russia said they'd take them if the U.S. gave Russia ten grand for each man and he was clothed from head to foot. What did they do to us? We served our time and they kicked us out. It's double jeopardy, that's what it is."

"It's triple jeopardy," said somebody else.

"They got five hundred Italians working at the Navy PX and warehouses. Why don't they give us Americans a chance to work?"

We had to move on to another restaurant because the police had received word the deportees were holding a meeting.

"They hound us night and day," said Mr. Di Marzo.

At the next restaurant, which was slightly darker, Joe the Wop said, "This is the way we feel about America. They done us harm; we done them harm. I come to America in my mother's arms. My father was a pioneer. Maybe I *was* the black sheep of my family. But if I become bad, America taught me to be bad. But I'm an American through and through. If you cut my insides out, you'll only find American blood. I never made no attempt to overthrow the American government."

"We might of committed crime," said Little Joe, "but we never was Communists."

"All I did," said Joe the Wop, "was live like a New Yorker. Laws were made to break. So we broke them, and if we got caught we got jailed. But this sending us back to Italy, that's something else again."

"You know why we're in Italy?" said Pop. "It's because there's no Italian big shots in America that will do anything for us. But we love America. Every time Old Glory is flying off one of them ships in the harbour, tears come to my eyes."

Several of the men said they had attempted to jump on ships and get back to the United States as stowaways, but very few ever made it. Blackie Joe said he was going to be reunited with his family no matter what happened. Several others also expressed a determination to get back one way or another.

"That's the only thing we hold on for," said Mr. Raimondo. "That and waiting to see Frank Frigenti again."

We had to move again from the restaurant in which we were eating because my hosts were afraid the police would arrive.

"You know what we want?" said Joe the Wop, when we were able to sit down again. "We want a pension from the United States. They owe it to us. The Italians owe us nothing."

"How much would you like?" I asked him.

"We think fifty dollars a month would be fair. We have families in America who pay taxes. Why shouldn't we get a little of it? They're giving millions of dollars to Italy and why don't we get any of it?"

"Why don't they send us to Alaska?" asked Mr. Raimondo. "We could work there. We would work like hell if they sent us. We'd shoot the first guy who wouldn't work."

"Even Ike said those lousy immigration laws should be thrown into the Hudson River," said Mr. Di Marzo.

"When he got sick, we was going to send him a spray of flowers," said Pop, "to wish him godspeed and remind him about the deportees down here. But we couldn't raise the money."

"The money just wasn't there," said Blackie Joe.

The only sources of income for deportees, as far as I could tell, came from escorting sailors around Naples and taking occasional excursions into contraband cigarettes and other American commodities. Naples is one of the great contraband cities of the world. But getting in contraband requires money, and there is a strict cash policy among contrabanders which makes it hard for a deportee to operate.

"I thought you fellows were given money by the combination," I said.

"That's a big, fat lie," said Mr. Di Marzo. "The combination gave us nothing. If we wanted to, we could take care of those big guys. We could bury them if we wanted to. We got guts. I'd like to see some of the guys in the combination go through what we've been through."

"I'd like to see Mr. Luciano," I said. "How do I get in touch with him?"

"Luciano? Luciano?" said Mr. Raimondo. "The name

rings a bell. Now where would I have heard it before?"

"I think there was a Luciano in Naples," said Pop. "But I don't recall him."

All the men at the table racked their brains to see if they could remember a man named Lucky Luciano.

"Seems to me," said Joe the Wop, "that a guy named Luciano used to own a candy store in my neighbourhood in the Bronx, but that's the only one I ever heard of."

I took a chance and went out to the race track, where who should I run into but Lucky himself! He was having a very unlucky time with the horses.

Mr. Luciano, who was under what is known as admonition in Naples, had to be off the streets at six o'clock at night. He could not associate with known criminals, had to stay out of bars, could not leave the city limits of Naples and had to report continually to the police.

"Are you happy?" I asked him.

"Why should I be?" he replied.

"I hear you've opened a surgical-supply house."

"Yeah. I'm selling operating tables, dentist chairs, X-ray machines and anaesthesia equipment. Here is my business card. I have all of southern Italy and Sicily as my territory. I got the franchise; the only ones who've given me real competition is the Germans."

"Do you know anything about the business?"

"No. But I'll learn. I'll have to if I want to branch out. It's a good business."

Mr. Luciano seemed to be the wealthiest of all deportees. He had a private income, lived in a five-room penthouse and even had his own business. But he found Naples as uncomfortable as the other deportees.

I asked him if he, like the others, would prefer to be in jail in the United States rather than a free man in Naples, and he replied, "Who's free in Naples?"

I MARCHED WITH THE REDS

Congress is bound to find out about this sooner or later so I might as well get it on record that I once marched in an East Berlin Communist May Day parade. It really wasn't my idea, but at the time it seemed like a good one, and I hope the people who frown on such things will hear me out.

Since I was in Berlin for May Day I naturally was interested in attending two large-scale celebrations, one held in the West sector by the Socialists, and one in the East sector by the Communists.

My loyalties have always been with the West, so I attended their celebration first. I stood for an hour with 400,000 West Berliners while the mayor and other distinguished guests denounced the Soviet Union in no uncertain terms.

After a respectable lapse of time, curiosity got the best of me, and I decided to go over to the East sector to see their parade and rally. But not knowing how the situation was at the Brandenburg Gate I sneaked into the East sector through the back streets around the gutted Reichstag building and over two dozen rubble-strewn blocks. As a precaution I ripped off my tie (the first mark of a capitalist), tried to rumple my suit and kicked up enough dust to dirty my shoes. In this disguise I hoped to look like a loyal East Berlin worker.

Pretty soon I started to hear the blaring of a voice over an amplifier. I followed the sound of the voice and came out on a street covered with banners and flags and crowded with people all walking towards what I presumed to be the rallying point. I joined the crowd and walked down the street for perhaps three blocks when the mob turned left and I suddenly found myself on Unter den Linden, which was formerly Berlin's Fifth Avenue, and now is East Berlin's favourite parade thoroughfare.

Unfortunately the mob at this point became an orderly group of marchers, and before I knew it I was parading down Unter den Linden with the workers of the world. I tried to escape, but both sides of the boulevard were lined with East German policemen and -women, and from the looks on their faces they were there to see that no one left the parade. One young German boy tried to get out and he was thrown right back in with the marchers and told to stay there.

Under the circumstances, I had no choice but to remain in the parade and join in the cheers. I looked around and found myself sandwiched between the East Berlin transport workers and an organization of Communist Youth, who were wearing uniforms of brown shirts and blue pants. The Communist youths looked far more dangerous than the transport workers, who for the most part seemed bored.

As I marched down Unter den Linden the loud-speaker blared out denunciations and cheers. The man at the mike would say down with American imperialism, and the marchers in the parade were supposed to answer "*Hoch! Hoch! Hoch!*"

The first time the man over the loud-speaker spoke, I kept my mouth shut, but a ten-year-old Communist youth marching next to me looked at me suspiciously. I smiled at him, but he didn't smile back. He gave me a small red flag and I took it gratefully, waving it to the crowds on the sidelines.

The next time the voice came over the loud-speaker it said something about NATO. This time I yelled as loud as I could, "*Hoch! Hoch! Hoch!*" Once again I erred. I was the only person yelling. A friend told me later in the day that the man on the mike had said in German that NATO wanted to take over the world.

Once again our ten-year-old friend looked at me suspiciously, and this time whispered something to another brown-shirted youth. I nervously fingered the red flag, waving it occasionally as I marched down the street.

By the time I had passed the famed Berlin University, I had denounced the Wall Street Warmongers, Konrad Adenauer, Yugoslavia and General Eisenhower. This last one was hard for me to do because while I was yelling "*Hoch! Hoch! Hoch!*" I was fingering two "I like Ike" buttons in my pants pockets. I cheered Russia ten times, Mao five, and the East Germany Plan for Peace five.

By now I was almost up to the tribune of honour. The gaily decorated reviewing stands were filled with pictures of Russian and German Communist heroes. Stalin, Marx and Lenin were given the most frequent tributes, but there was some room left for East Berlin Mayor Pieck and East German Prime Minister Grotewohl. We came up abreast of the tribune. The Communist youths straightened up and my ten-year-old friend indicated that I should do the same. As I passed, the young folks gave a salute and the transport workers waved. As I wasn't in uniform I decided the best thing to do was to wave also. Pieck waved back. I kept my little flag going as long as I thought it prudent and then relaxed.

At last the parade was over and we all broke up. I should have just taken off for the West sector immediately but I had a score to settle. As the crowd was dispersing I went up to my ten-year-old friend, gave him back his red flag and said in English, "The Communists are the real warmongers."

Then I hoch-footed it into the crowd before he could catch me. The little stinker never knew what hit him.

THE BALLHAUS RESI BAR

ONE OF THE more intriguing cabarets in Europe is Berlin's Ballhaus Resi Bar. The Resi, which has been a Berlin institution for thirty years, was originally located on the Blumenstrasse in what is now the Russian sector of the city. The old building was destroyed during the war and last year the owner, Paul Baatz, built a new Resi in West Berlin, near Tempelhof Airport.

When I went to the cabaret, Mr. Baatz, an agile man of seventy, was kind enough to show me around.

The cabaret, which handles between 1,200 and 1,500 people at a time, is about the size and shape of a large aircraft hangar. It has two hundred table-booths and attached to each booth is a telephone. There is also a lighted number over the booth so someone at another table knows what number to call.

In the front is a large bandstand for the dance orchestra and above it is a gigantic stage with the curtains closed.

The idea, of course, is for lonely men and lonely women to meet each other via the telephone. Everyone sits in his or her own booth waiting to get a call. Since there are usually more women than men at the Resi, the men who go there receive more calls.

Mr. Baatz let me call a table. I chose a heavy-set blonde at extension 456. She answered the phone and I was surprised to discover she spoke English. She said she would be glad to dance with me. I told her I was only trying out the system and she hung up with a bang.

I was ready to call another table, but Mr. Baatz told me the entertainment was going on. The show at the Resi consists entirely of water. The curtain in front of the giant stage opened and a great display of fountains sprang up from the floor. The fountains danced to a waltz while coloured lights played on them.

This fountain display lasted for nine minutes and was certainly unlike any cabaret show I had ever seen before. As soon as the curtain fell, the phones started ringing again and men and women from different tables got up to dance.

Besides his telephones and his fountains, Mr. Baatz has a pneumatic system whereby people can send written messages to each other via a tube. The central office for the *pneumatique* is located in the back of the club and here one or two girls censor the messages and send them on to the correct tables. Mr. Baatz has a rule that no improper messages and no political messages can be sent via the system.

He took me into the booth where the censoring was done and introduced me to a young girl named Renate Gerhold, who said she was a coed at the Frei University and worked nights to pay her way. She pulled out a cigar box full of unprintable messages. "Usually we tear them up," she said, "but some of them we save for fun."

Mr. Baatz said I could stay with Miss Gerhold and read some of the messages that were coming through. I copied down a few:

A lady at table 407 wrote to a man at table 224:

"I love you, I will always love you. Where is your love for me? Please call me."

A soldier at table 324 sent a message to a girl at table 267: "Hey, baby, you with the brunette hair and pearl earrings, how's about a dance with a real man?"

The message from 267 came back a few minutes later: "I'm not your baby, but I'd love to dance with a real man. I hope you are the tall soldier with moustache and not the half-pint sitting across from him."

A tube from table 412 confused me. It was meant for 380 and it said: "I am a jewel and you're crazy."

Then 289, a woman, wrote to 287: "My husband isn't here tonight. Do not be afraid to dance with me."

Two eighty-seven wrote back: "I'm not afraid of your husband. I just don't want to see you any more."

From 213 came a note to 346: "You never answered my note. You are cruel. I am not just a woman—I'm a lady."

The next one surprised me. A man from 243 wrote to a woman at 245: "I want to take you home with me tonight. I am a man of honour."

Miss Gerhold was going to send it on and I said, "You're not going to send that one, are you?"

She replied, "Well, he said he was a man of honour, didn't he?"

A soldier at table 472 wrote his buddy at 456: "Hey, Meatball, how're the blondes?"

Meatball wrote back: "They can't dance and they can hardly speak English. Get me out of here."

Miss Gerhold was pretty cynical about her job. "They all write such stupid things. It's very boring work."

Just then a message from 419 came through with a pornographic sketch. She showed it to me without so much as a blush and tore it up.

"I can't understand people at all," she said.

Mr. Baatz came back to get me. He said he had new plans for the next few months. He was going to institute a service whereby people could send cognac, flowers and frankfurters to each other via the *pneumatique*. Mr. Baatz said it was easier to impress a girl with a gift than a note, and besides, it was quite a profitable concession.

"Many of these couples you see out there are children of people who met each other at the Resi Bar. Before the war people were a lot more vulgar than they are now. The Resi today is a family institution and we plan to keep it that way."

I made a few telephone calls, but all the lines were busy, so I said good-bye to Mr. Baatz and went home alone.

BONA FIDE LEG-PULLERS

"WE'RE TRYING to get more tourists to come to Ireland," the man from the tourist office said. "We'd like to get Americans and we'd be much obliged if they would spend some dollars with us."

"What does Ireland have to offer?"

"That's a good question and I thank you for asking it. Ireland has closer ties with America than probably any nation in Europe. There are about twenty million people of Irish descent in the United States, and I think there's a bond between us that no other country can claim.

"We don't even think of Americans as tourists. To most Irishmen, they're 'visitors', and since the average Irishman thinks the only ones who make any money on tourists are hotel keepers, they don't regard Americans as commercial prospects. Therefore, as a visitor, they must give him courtesy. Since the American isn't treated like a tourist, he enjoys being one."

"Aren't the Irish great ones for pulling an American's leg?"

"That's a good question and I thank you for asking it. You see, there is a certain type of American who wants to know about leprechauns, fairies and the like, and who treats the Irish like the Little People.

"Now when that type arrives, the Irish feel it is only fair to pull the fellow's leg in all directions.

"Leg-pulling is not just aimed at the Americans. There's nothing an Irishman likes to do better than pull an Englishman's leg. The Yanks are much more with us than the English, and the Irish are always willing to see how far they can go in egging an Englishman on.

"During the war the poor British correspondents who came over here wrote some very imaginative pieces based

C

on things they were told in the more imaginative pubs.
You might say they were taken to the cleaners."

I received a small sample of the great Irish oral tradition and the great Irish art of leg-pulling when a friend
took me to a pub with Stanton Deleplane, a San Francisco
scribe. We no sooner had our drinks when a man who
introduced himself as Liam Boyd said, "You're Americans
aren't you?"

We said we were.

"Then you'd be interested in knowing that only a few
yards from here lived the great Tammany Hall American
politician, Boss Richard Croker."

"Did he?"

"Aye, he won the Derby with a horse named Orby. He
was a multimillionaire. They say he was married to a half-
Indian woman named Beulah. When he died in 1916 he
was buried standing up in between the front door of his
house."

"That's not true," someone else said. "I heard it from
Paddy MacKnight he was buried horizontal in the front
door."

Another guest disagreed. "Sarah O'Toole was invited
to the funeral and she said he was buried in a baking tin
in the back yard."

Mr. Boyd said, "It was the front door and he was buried
standing up. When the O'Neils moved in, Mrs. O'Neil
couldn't stand the thought of Boss Croker standing in the
door every time she went by. Finally they took the whole
door off and buried it in the family cemetery."

"I've lived here forty years," another man said, "and
I know for a fact that Boss Croker was buried down in the
cellar, and he was buried horizontal."

The question of which direction Boss Croker was buried
was kicked back and forth for an hour.

"You sure it wasn't Orby the horse that was buried in

the front door?" the bartender asked. "Seems to me it was a pretty big door and Croker said he always wanted to have Orby buried standing up."

"No. Orby was buried in the cemetery, lying down. There's a marker stating the fact."

"But the way I heard it, the O'Neils were very disturbed. Someone must have been buried in the door. There's no way of a man being buried in such a door horizontally. But he could have been buried diagonally."

The lads in the pub thought we were getting a little bored with Boss Croker, and they said, "Would you like to hear about leprechauns?"

We said no, we didn't plan on leaving the pub until we got to the bottom of Boss Croker's burial.

"I've got it on final authority," said the postman, "that Boss Croker was buried in America right in the centre of the bar in Tammany Hall."

It was a great discussion and although they pulled our legs all evening, we didn't even need crutches when we finally decided to go home.

VENICE À LA HEMINGWAY

EVERY PERSON who comes to Venice is influenced in some way by one of the great writers who have written about the city. Hemingway has probably influenced me more than anyone, and without *Across the River and into the Trees*, I doubt if I'd even have enjoyed being there.

Take, for example, the night when I went to dinner at the Gritti Palace Hotel with my wife. It was a good dinner, an imposing dinner, a lobster dinner, and the lobster he was good. When he arrived he was dark and green and unfriendly and cost a day's wages, but when they grilled him he was red and I wouldn't have traded five suits for him.

I looked across the table at my wife. She looked good. Almost as good as the lobster. "She looks as lovely as a gondola," I thought to myself, "or Stan Musial or Joe DiMaggio. She could drive a home run into the canal if I let her." I held her hand tightly. "I love you and I'm glad you're you," I told her. "Daughter, let's go for a ride in a gondola after dinner."

"What is this daughter business?" my wife said. "And stop holding my hand so tight. I can't eat my lobster."

"My poor daughter, my little daughter, my only daughter," I said. "Who do you love?"

"If you call me daughter once more," my wife said, "I'm going to hit you with this bottle of wine. And while you're in this mood, would you mind telling me what you were doing all afternoon on the beach with Gina Lollobrigida?"

"Moon is my mother and father," I told her. "A lobster fills with the moon. When he is dark he is not worth eating, little daughter."

"I wasn't talking about the lobster," she said. "I was talking about Lollobrigida."

"Please, daughter. You must try to understand my attitude. When you have killed so many you can afford to be a little wild."

"How many have you killed?"

"One hundred and eighty sures, not counting possibles."

"And you have no remorse?"

"None."

"Well, I do, and you'd better watch your step."

"Come, daughter, come, let's not think of Lollobrigida. We will find a gondola and you will be you and I will be me and the gondolier will be him."

"I'm warning you about this daughter business."

We walked outside. Now she looked more like Mickey Mantle or a young Bobby Feller. What a pitcher she'd make, I thought.

We found a gondola which was long and good and brave and true and it was our gondola for as long as we wanted it, for that's how it is in Venice. A man can either take a gondola or leave it alone. Only tourists and lovers take gondolas in Venice, I thought. Tourists and lovers and people who can afford them. Where does that leave me?

"Why can't we take a motorboat?" my wife asked. "A gondola is awfully slow."

"Because you're my wife and we're alone and it is Venice and I want to hold you close and I want you to hold me close and anyway it's cheaper than taking a motorboat."

"The canal smells," she said.

"So does war. So do the Russians. So do lobsters and garlic and perfume. Everything smells, daughter. We've just got to get used to it. Have you ever skied in the dark?"

"Listen. I'm getting sick of this nonsense. Let's go back to the Lido and see one of the movies. You came down for the film festival."

"The pictures smell almost as much as the canal. Except for Marlon Brando and Cary Grant and Frank Sinatra and some selected short subjects, I'd rather be in a gondola with you."

"The Italian starlets seem to have attracted your attention."

"They're nothing compared to the 'Star-Spangled Banner' or baby shrimps at the Taverna or sole at the Colombo or you at first base for the New York Yankees. I looked at them as I would look at any live animals in the jungle. Let's go to Harry's for one last drink before I kiss you once and for all forever and for a day."

"I want to go back to the hotel," my wife said. "The gondola or the lobster have made me sick."

"Which one, daughter?"

"How the hell do I know?"

"All right, I'll take you home and read you Dante and tell you about war and the Krauts and the very brave boys and guys like Pete Quesada and Red Smith and the Montana National Guard. Now before you get sick, daughter, kiss me and love me straight and true."

It must have been the last "daughter," because before I knew it I was in the canal with all my clothes on. But it was good to be alive and wet and in love and in Venice. Hemingway couldn't have had a better time.

REACHING THE SUMMIT

EVERY PERSON in Europe has his favourite winter sport. Some like to ski, others ice skate, and still others bobsled. My favourite winter sport is social climbing. Ever since I can remember I've been hacking away at the diamond peaks of international society, planting the American flag in the mink coats and thick skulls of some of the most important people in the world.

It isn't that I social climb for myself (though heaven knows I need the exercise), but I do it for my wife's sake. She was cheated out of a title by marriage, and although she never says anything about it, every once in a while I can see that faraway look in her eyes, as if she's saying, "If I hadn't married him, I wonder if I would have been the ex-Queen of Egypt."

I've tried to make it up to her by taking her to places where people who are people go. In the summer we go to Monte Carlo, Cannes and Deauville. In the winter we go to St. Moritz, Belgrade and Zagreb, and while it isn't the same thing as being the ex-Queen of Egypt, it's better than living in Brooklyn.

For Christmas I decided to take my wife to one of the most exclusive places in Europe, the Mittersill Castle and Hunting Club, located just outside Kitzbühel, Austria. The Mittersill Club is owned and run by Baron Hubert Pantz and Prince Alexander Hohenlohe for the benefit of the underprivileged rich. It has less than one hundred members, equally divided between the European and North American continents, who like to hunt their stag and chamois in privacy, and prefer the easygoing castle life to the harsh Grand Hotel life that so many of them have become used to.

In choosing Mittersill for Christmas I was taking two chances. There was a good chance they wouldn't let us in, and a better chance that we would be arrested for trespassing. But those are the risks one takes when one climbs the dangerous social mountain range of Europe.

I had a plan. We could go to Kitzbühel and wait for a snowstorm. Then, with the snow pouring down, we would go to the castle and ask to stay for the night. Once we were in the place, my wife was to break her leg and then they would have to let us stay. (I always take a hammer along with me when I go to a winter resort.)

The first snowfall came the day before Christmas. We left Kitzbühel and arrived at the castle just after dark. It was a forbidding-looking place. I had heard that the castle was built in the twelfth century and was used as a fortress guarding the countryside's emerald mines. There were over a hundred rooms and three dungeons, where they used to boil witches in big pots. This practice was discontinued when Baron Pantz and Prince Hohenlohe took over. Ghosts are still said to linger there, but they only have to pay half price and they usually take their meals in their rooms.

I knocked on the door. It was answered by Prince Hohenlohe.

"We were caught in a snowstorm," I said. "Kind sir, please could my wife and I sleep in the stable?"

The prince frowned. "There is no room in the stable; you'll have to sleep in the house." He let us in.

"This is a private club," the prince told us. "But you can stay for the night. I hope you brought your black tie and evening clothes."

"Oh, yes, I always carry them when I expect to get lost in the snow."

He made me sign the guest book. "You wouldn't be related to any of the royal family, would you?" he said hopefully.

"I've heard it said," I replied, "that one of my ancestors was the idiot son of Henri le Fou. Will that help?"

"It will have to do," he said. "Please don't think I'm stuffy, but you see our membership lists include Prince Bernhard of the Netherlands, the Earl of Hardwicke, Prince Peter of Yugoslavia, the Maharaja and Maharani of Jaipur, Sir Francis and Lady Peel, Princess Troubetzkoy and Spyros Skouras. In the sixteenth century the peasants attacked the castle and made such a mess of things that we haven't let the peasant stock in since."

It was perfectly understandable.

That night being Christmas, we had a wonderful dinner. Afterward, we exchanged gifts. We gave the other guests warm glances. They gave us icy stares.

We sang the old Christmas favourites: "I Caught the Princess of Hohenlohe Kissing Santa Claus," "Sir Santa Claus Is Coming to Town," "Dashing Through the Snow in a 14-Carat Sled" and "Roll Out the Royces."

As the evening wore on everyone warmed up. When Prince Hohenlohe revealed that I was descended from the idiot son of Henri le Fou, the guests showed some interest in me, and when my wife lifted a dining-room chair with her teeth, I knew we were in.

At the end of the evening Prince Hohenlohe told me, "The other members like you and they think we should make you a member. The life membership is one thousand dollars. Would you care to pay tonight, so you can sleep with a clear conscience?"

I gave him the thousand dollars gladly.

When we got back to the room we hugged each other, we were so happy.

"They liked us," my wife said gleefully. "And you didn't even have to break my leg."

I put the hammer away. We had reached the Mount Everest of social climbing, and there was no place to go from Mittersill but down.

THE GREAT GRIMALDI FEUD

MANY PEOPLE, particularly members of the British press, expressed surprise at the cool reception I received at the hands of the Monegasque royal family.

"We can understand it for ourselves," they told me, "but how can they snub somebody like you—somebody who got into the Mittersill Hunting Club?"

The answer is quite simple. I was snubbed at Monaco for one simple reason. The Buchwalds and the Grimaldis (the royal house of Monaco) have not spoken to each other since January 8, 1297.

The reason for the feud is lost somewhere in the cobwebs of history, but it was at a time when one of my ancestors, then working for the Viking News Service, covered a battle that Rainier Grimaldi fought against the Flemish Navy. Rainier I, then an admiral, decreed that only members of the Associated, United and International Press associations could accompany him into battle, but my ancestor, disguised as a Genoese sailor, hid on board the flagship and scooped the other three news agencies by four years.

In 1523, when Lucien Grimaldi, son of Lambert, and successor to his brother Jean II, was assassinated by his nephew, Barthelemy Doria, the palace tried to hush the news up. But an alert ancestor of mine, then working for the *Volga Free Press*, broke the story and prevented Barthelemy from sitting on the throne.

And so it's gone down through history. There was talk that Charlotte de Grammont, daughter of the Marshal de

Grammont, who married the Duke of Valentinois on April 28, 1659, was in love with Rudolph Buchwald, then a court reporter for the *News of the World*. But we only have Rudolph's diary as evidence, and every one in the family knows how unreliable he was.

You won't find a page in the history of Monaco where a Buchwald hasn't offended a Grimaldi or a Grimaldi hasn't offended a Buchwald. Generation after generation the families have stayed clear of each other.

Just last year, my Aunt Molly from Brooklyn was making up her guest list for my cousin Joseph's wedding to a nice girl from Flatbush.

I suggested she invite Prince Rainier, who was then in the United States.

"No Grimaldis," she said, "will be allowed at Joseph's wedding."

"But Aunt Molly," I protested, "this is the twentieth century. We've got to forget ancient family feuds. Prince Rainier's a nice fellow."

"I don't care for myself," Aunt Molly said, "but you know what a long memory your Uncle Oscar has. Besides, has Prince Rainier invited Joseph to his wedding?"

No matter how much I tried to persuade Aunt Molly, she wouldn't send the Prince an invitation to Joseph's wedding. How he found out about it I'll never know, but as soon as I received that cool reception in Monaco, I knew Aunt Molly had made a mistake. The Grimaldis still had it in for the Buchwalds.

I can understand Prince Rainier's attitude toward us, but I can't understand the Kelly family behaving the way they have. The Buchwalds have always liked the Kellys. Back when Mr. Kelly senior was turned down at Henley, my father sent a telegram to the King and said, "If Jack Kelly can't row at Henley, then I won't row either."

So what happened at Monte Carlo? Mr. and Mrs. Kelly threw a dinner for the bridal party at the Monte

Carlo Casino, and do you know where I was? I was outside in the rain holding a flashlight for a photographer
from a Finnish newspaper. That's the thanks my father
got for sending the telegram to the King of England.

I RAN WITH THE HARES

A MAN'S SEARCH for what to do with his leisure time
goes on and on in Europe. In England people like to go
punting, in Spain they like to kill bulls, in Switzerland
they like to make fondue, and in France they like to watch
governments fall. But the Irish, who are just about a race
apart from everybody else, like to spend their weekdays
hunting foxes and their Sundays following beagles.

Whereas horse racing is the recreation of kings, beagling
is the pastime of the common people and of those sports-
men who are afraid of losing their seats. All one needs is
a pair of legs, a pack of hounds and a frightened hare. The
object of the sport is to chase the hounds on foot over hill
and dale while they pursue a hare. There is very little
chance of the beagles catching the hare and less chance
of the beaglers catching the beagles.

Then, says the cynical sportsman, where's the pay-off?
The pay-off comes, as J. Ivester Lloyd, an expert on
beagling, explains, when "you find yourself laughing as
you splash, knee-deep, through a cold brook, flounder in
the trodden mire of a gateway, tear your clothes on
brambles, or get hung up on a strand of barbed wire.
Why do people beagle? The question is ridiculous. For
once anyone has really taken to the sport it becomes
almost second nature, a part of his or her make-up. To
ask why of a beagler would be like asking a normal man
why he eats or breathes."

I was invited to go beagling one Sunday afternoon on Ted O'Connor's farm about eighteen miles out of Dublin. Ted O'Connor owns about four hundred acres of very fertile Irish land that is divided up by barbed-wire fences, tangled brush, deep gullies and heavy undergrowth. It is what is known as perfect beagling country.

The beagles were of the famous Goldburn pack. They were owned by an Englishman who trains beagles for pleasure and who travels hundreds of miles every Sunday to lead the beaglers in pursuit of the hounds.

We all gathered in front of O'Connor's gatehouse at two o'clock. There were seven pairs of beagles, three kennel huntsmen and forty-five followers of the chase bundled up in sweaters and scarves and all wearing long rubber boots or galoshes. A few people were wearing gloves, but that was the only equipment that we were allowed. The master of the hounds shook hands all around. Then he sounded a note on his horn, the dogs let out their yelps and away we went, noses to the ground, in search of a hare.

Every once in a while the master let go with a "Yipe Yipe Yipe-it" to give the beagles encouragement. The first field we came to looked as if it were covered with brown oatmeal. We all sank gently into the ground up to our noses as the beagles trotted on in search of the scent. Eventually I made it to a barbed-wire fence and climbed over, ripping only one sleeve to shreds. This, commented some of the other followers, was very good, considering I was only out for the first time.

Suddenly there was a loud hallo! The beagles found a hare and the chase was on. The second field we dashed through looked like green cream of wheat and the third resembled a day-old bowl of corn flakes. Untangling myself from a gully full of thorns, in which I ripped the other sleeve, I crawled to the top of a hill where I watched as the hounds gave pursuit. The hare was way out in front and didn't seem worried about the chase. Suddenly he doubled back and came straight at me.

I made a dive for him, but he managed to escape. I expected to get complimented for a good try, but instead the master and the followers gave me a dressing down. "In beagling," the master said, his face red with fury, "the followers must never interfere with the hare. The beagles are the only ones who may try to catch him."

Ted O'Connor apologized for me and said it wouldn't happen again, and the chase recommenced. Over hedge and stile, ploughed and fallow, I ran in pursuit. I feathered along furrows, and almost plucked a plover. "Huick, huick," cried the master. I tripped over a spiky stump, ran back across the brown oatmeal field, which now in the dimming afternoon looked and felt more like thick green pea soup. A branch cut my forehead, part of my pants was left on barbed wire, and part of my right ear was left in a tree. Yet the merry chorus of the pack and the shouting of the master drove me on.

The hounds were just about to catch the hare when he ran for cover; the scent was lost and all of us, panting and shouting with excitement, wallowed in the green cream of wheat while the beagles sniffed disconsolately around.

It was too dark to look any further and we all went back to O'Connor's house for tea and to sew our clothes back together again.

Why do people do it? It's hard to say. For me it's enough to be in the company of beagles and be with cheery folks who enjoy the sport as much as I do. I've become a confirmed beagler. But it won't be as much fun next time. Since I left my right ear on that tree I won't be able to hear the beagles picking up the scent very well and that, as most beaglers will tell you, is 99 per cent of the fun.

WHITE HUNTER, RED FOX

NOT LONG AFTER my baptism of beagling, Mr. John Huston, the movie director, who lives the life of Riley in Ireland between pictures, invited me to join him at his country estate one week-end to ride the hounds and hunt the foxes with the landed gentry of County Kildare.

When I arrived Mr. Huston gave the butler my bags and took me into the library. "Now, sit down, kid, I want to talk to you."

"Yes, sir, Mr. Huston."

"Now, kid, what exactly do you know about fox hunting?"

"Well, I've been reading up on it and Oscar Wilde said that fox hunting is the pursuit of the inedible by the unspeakable."

Mr. Huston blanched. "That's just what I was afraid of. As long as you're going to be with us I think we'd better get you straight on fox hunting. Once you understand it, you'll realize what a wonderful thing fox hunting really is."

"Yes, sir."

"Fox hunting is one of the greatest and roughest sports in the world," Mr. Huston said. "It is the real test of horsemanship, sportsmanship and woodmanship. And Irish fox hunting is the best fox hunting of all."

"Why don't they just shoot the foxes and be done with it?" I asked.

"Because, kid, the only time you can shoot a fox is at night, and nine chances out of ten the farmer will only wound him and he will die a cruel, lingering death. In fox hunting, once the fox is trapped, he is entitled to a quick, clean death."

"Why don't they gas them? That would do it."

"You're missing the point. The fox serves a great purpose. The Irish people don't want to kill all the foxes. The fox is Ireland's best friend. If it weren't for the fox there would be no great breed of Irish horses, those big-boned, heavy-muscled, bold, noble creatures who are responsible for the great steeplechase races throughout the world.

"And by the same token the fox is responsible for producing the great courage in Irish people. My boy, you haven't lived until you've seen an Irish woman, sixty-five or seventy years old, sitting side-saddle on a horse, and taking one of the great Irish banks. The Irish love their fox hunting so much that every year a half-dozen oldsters fall out of their saddles and are dead before they hit the ground. They literally die with their boots on. ᐧ

"And, oh, the women! The world owes a debt to the Irish women and to fox hunting. The Irish women are the mothers of Ireland's greatest export—Irishmen. I would go so far as to say that Guinness Stout and fox hunting are responsible for most of the good characteristics in Irishmen."

"What is responsible for the bad ones?" I asked.

"Irish whiskey. But don't change the subject. Not only is fox hunting a humane sport, but it gives the fox a chance to get away. A fox is caught only one out of four times. Now what could be fairer?"

"Maybe if they imported a fox blight of some sort it would kill them off in no time," I said.

"People say," said Mr. Huston, "that fox hunting is a posh sport only for toffs, but I would say it was one of the most democratic sports there is. Anyone who can ride a horse is welcome to join in a fox hunt. This isn't just true of Ireland, it's true everywhere."

I disagreed. "I had an uncle in Brooklyn who tried to join a fox hunt on Long Island, and the people set the hounds on him. Chased him all the way back to Brooklyn."

Mr. Huston was becoming annoyed. "Look, kid, once

you're out in the field on a horse you'll feel differently about this. I am going to take you on a fox hunt tomorrow and you'll see for yourself exactly what I have been talking about. Now, are there any more questions?"

"Well, there is one. Why don't they set out poison? It seems that would really knock them off."

For the first time Mr. Huston looked as if he was sorry he asked me to come along.

The following morning was "a grand, soft day," which means in Ireland that it was raining like hell. Originally, I had planned to wear a cowboy suit with two ·45-calibre revolvers around my waist. But when the master of the hunt saw this he made me go back and change. I was given instead a pink swallow-tailed coat, yellow vest, white tie, black boots and a tall black silk hat. They wouldn't even let me keep my revolvers.

The horse Mr. Huston had selected for me was a large, grey stallion named Lots of Lolly, a raring beast no different from any other jumping horse except that it talked a blue streak. Now there are people who say horses don't talk and it's true in most of the world. But Ireland, a country haunted by ghosts, inhabited by leprechauns and driven mad by banshees, is the exception. Horses not only talk here; you can't keep them quiet.

"You ever been fox hunting before?" Lots of Lolly asked.

"No, sir," I honestly replied.

"I thought so," he said. "You really haven't a very good seat. Well, if you're game, I guess I am. But try to behave yourself. Don't pull on my mouth, and throw that damned whip away. Just leave everything to me."

We had some time to wait before the hunt began and Lots of Lolly seemed very bored. "Say, did ya hear the one about . . ."

"Hounds, gentlemen, please," the master of the hunt said, and the whipper-ins, with the hounds neatly packed together, moved down to the first covert.

"What are they doing now?" I asked Lots of Lolly.

"Just wait. There, now the fox is going away, the hounds have the scent and they're giving tongue. Now the master is blowing 'Gone Away' on his horn and the hunt is on. Let's go."

I started off with Lots of Lolly trying to take the lead. The master of hunt's face became contorted. "If you please, sir, would you mind staying in the field?"

"Don't let him talk to you like that," Lots of Lolly said. "Are we hunting or are we not hunting? He's just a big bag of kale." I was just about to tell the master of the hunt he was a bag of kale when the first bank loomed up in front of us.

"Close your eyes," Lots of Lolly said, "let go of the reins and leave everything to me."

I closed my eyes but couldn't help peeping. When I saw what was in front of me I shrieked. Lots of Lolly became furious. "I told you to shut your eyes—or would you prefer that I shut them for you?"

I shut them and Lots of Lolly soared beautifully over the bank, landing on all fours on the other side of the ditch.

"You see?" he said. "What did I tell you? Now let's hear the music of the hounds."

We turned and headed for the woods. Lots of Lolly was running three strides ahead of the rest of the hunt. Suddenly I looked ahead and saw a bank slightly higher than Mount Everest.

Lots of Lolly shuddered. "Do you see what I see?"

"Yes, sir."

"Are you willing to take a chance?"

"Yes, sir," I said as we approached the jump.

"Well," said Lots of Lolly, "I'm not."

And with that he stopped abruptly and threw me out of the saddle, over the bank into the water-filled ditch, and then, snickering with pleasure, galloped away.

Two hours later, while I was still swimming around in the mud, Lots of Lolly came back with the brush between his teeth. "You certainly missed a wonderful hunt," he said.

"What happened?"

"Well, we found a fox at Palmerstown which went to ground near the house. We went to Forenaughts, where we had a nice thirty minutes. At Tipperhaven, the hounds drew ferness, where the fox left immediately and going for the kill he swung right-handed through Major Mainguy's bottoms leaving Arthurstown on his right. The hounds killed in the open, just short of Kilteal Finish. And because I got there first, they gave me the brush. You should have come along; you would have loved it."

"Would you give me a ride back to town?" I asked him.

"With all that filthy goop on you? I should say not. What kind of horse do you think I am, anyhow?"

I told him, and Lots of Lolly went away mad.

TAMING THE THAMES

THAMES RIVER society—as I can assure you, because I've successfully crashed it—is divided into three classes: those that row, those that paddle and those that punt. Of the three, the punting people are the most numerous, and the sport, which seems to have caught on only in England, is revered from pole to pole. A punt is a long, narrow, flat-bottomed boat squared at both ends and propelled along the river by a person in an upright position who pushes herself with a pole. This leisurely method of transportation has several features that make it particularly attractive to sporting people. One is that each stroke is different from the previous one, depending, of course, on the depth as well as the hardness and softness of the river bottom, and you don't have to put up with the monotony of the regularity of the rowing stroke.

Secondly, punting allows the person to see where she is going, which rowing and sculling do not do. There are some people who will argue that they don't care to see where they're going as long as they get there, but punters are forward-looking and they always have their eyes on the horizon.

The third and most important argument for punting is that it is an ideal form of exercise for a woman, and the male, who is usually forced to pull his oars in a rowing boat, can relax in the well of the stern while his lady friend pushes and pulls the punt along at a quiet and easy pace.

As a matter of fact, A. H. Grubb, in his book *Rowing, Sculling, Canoeing and Punting*, is all for women punters and says: "There is no more graceful picture imaginable than a charming young girl propelling her craft on the river with ease and grace."

Mr. Grubb, whose book was a great help to my wife during her novice period on the Thames, points out that there are two methods of punting. There is the Old Short Stroke method, where violence is a great factor in success, and the new modern Long Shove Method, developed in 1877 by Abel Beasley at Oxford. Mr. Beasley was to punting what W. G. Grace was to cricket, a champion through and through.

Beasley wasn't a man to just grab a pole and start pushing. He studied punting from the bottom up, and when he had finally perfected the long shove, there wasn't a man on the Thames who could come near him. His secret was to keep his body upright instead of bending over the pole, where much of the punter's weight is lost. Beasley worked from the loins and finished his stroke well out, a motion which startled and defeated his competitors.

No punter worth her salt goes out on the Thames today

without first saying, "Well done, Beasley!" and making her first long shove in honour of the father of modern-day punting.

Grubb points out that the proper way to stand in a punt is to keep your face forward and your feet about twelve inches apart—but not too far, or you may lose your balance. The toes should not be in too straight a line forward, though they must point in the direction in which you are going. Your eyes should be on the bow and if you are travelling fast you must drop the pole well in front of you.

Since there is no rudder on a punt you have to steer with the pole. This is done by pushing the pole against the side of the punt or away from it, depending on the direction in which you wish to go.

That's all there is to it, and once a woman learns the principles of punting all a decent man has to do is buy the Sunday papers and sit as quietly as possible in the well of the boat so he won't disturb its balance. As long as his wife holds a steady course and doesn't get the pole stuck in the mud there is no reason why the man should disturb himself at all. But if she makes mistakes when she first goes out, it is the duty of her husband to be tolerant. We all can't be Beasleys at the beginning and even women can make mistakes.

After letting my wife win her punting blue, I was invited to attend the Royal Regatta at Henley. As I knew it would bring back many happy memories of my sculling days in Central Park, I was very happy to go. But one doesn't just go to Henley—one prepares for it. As Jack Clyde, my amiable host, pointed out, "The Henley crowd is the only good crowd left in England and there are certain formalities expected of the spectators, just as there are certain things expected of the crews. A spectator, in order to fit in, must wear white flannels, a blazer, his school tie and

school cap, and any medals he may have won while
racing for his college or club."

And so, for a week prior to the event, my wife was busy
at work sewing brass buttons on my old navy suit and
embroidering the Central Park crest (two oars crossed,
with the words "Twenty-five Cents an Hour" in the centre)
over the left-hand pocket as well as on the cap. I didn't
have a school tie, but as luck would have it, I found a
green-and-red stripe at Sulka's, and those were exactly
the colours of Public School 35 in Hollis, New York. I
bought the white flannels at an antique shop and also
bought several medals at the Flea Market. Most of them
had to do with the Crimean War, but Clyde assured me
no one would scrutinize us that closely.

There are several places where you can watch the
Henley Regatta. There are the Stewards' Stands, the
boating tents, the yachts, or the famous boating clubs. I
was invited to Phyllis Court Club, which is so exclusive
that even the squirrels that frequent it have to wear
badges. The Phyllis Court Club overlooks Father Thames
just at the finishing line of the Regatta, and from its long
sweeping lawns and under its superb trees people have a
chance to forget about the other classes for a little while
and relax in the style that they are accustomed to.

There are two famous rowing festivals in England. One
is the Boat Race, the contest between Oxford and Cam-
bridge, and the other is the Henley Royal Regatta, which
welcomes, but does not always accept, competitors from
all over the world. Henley possesses what is probably the
finest stretch of water in the country.

The regatta was first organized in 1839 and has been
held annually ever since, usually during the first week in
July. The teams compete for silver cups. The two most
important are the Grand Challenge Cup, considered the
Blue Riband of eight-oared racing, and the Thames Challenge Cup, which has crossed the Atlantic after eleven out

of the last twelve meetings. There are also cups for four-oared crews, two-oared crews and the Diamond Challenge Sculls—unofficial amateur championship of the world—for solo scullers.

The course is a straight mile and five-sixteenths, and it is piled and boomed, whatever that means.

Saturday was the final day and there were many titanic struggles in the offing. The weather was warm and sultry and the water smooth and lazy. In the first race, the Princeton eight, America's only hope for the Thames Challenge Cup, was defeated by a stalwart crew from the RAF. All of us who saw it could not help shouting as the boats crossed the finish line, "Well rowed, RAF!"

In the Grand Challenge Cup, Leander, Britain's most famous rowing club, defeated the Union Sportive Métropolitaine des Transports from France in a thrilling race that brought out the best traditions of rowing. Even though the British Crew won, those of us who could speak French could not refrain from yelling, "Well rowed, Union Sportive Métropolitaine des Transports from France!"

In the Ladies Challenge Cup, Radley College and Jesus College fought it out and it was a brilliant, hard-fought race. Jesus College finally defeated Radley, and many of us shouted, "Well rowed! Well rowed!" carefully refraining from any blasphemy.

After the awards had been distributed, I went punting down the Thames and retired to my pub for a pint. It didn't take me long to discover that two pints equal one quart and four quarts equal a gallon.

Late in the evening I went back to the river to watch a fireworks display. Many people dressed in evening clothes for the Royal Regatta ball went out punting to see the fireworks and it was a very stirring sight and a very stirring finish to a very stirring day.

I don't wish to use these pages for commercial purposes

but if anyone is in the market for a pair of white flannels or a set of brass buttons or a rowing cap with a Central Park crest on it, please let me know. I'll even throw in an old school tie from Public School 35 if the price is right. As for the Crimean medals, I think I'll keep them. They can always come in handy for a Fourth of July cocktail or one of Perle Mesta's parties.

ORDEAL AT ASCOT

I KNOW IT'S POOR form to brag when one is in England, but when one goes to Ascot one likes to make a point of it. Ascot, for the uninitiated, is the only racecourse in England which belongs to the Crown. Founded by Good Queen Anne in 1711, Royal Ascot Week is the most important event on the social horseflesh calendar. Any blue-blooded Briton will tell you a visit to Ascot during Royal Ascot Week is "the thing to do."

But one doesn't just go to Ascot—one worries oneself sick making preparations for it. Rumour has it that Ascot is so exclusive that it is the only racecourse in the world where the horses own the people. One must be dressed to the teeth when one is in attendance. The only attire acceptable is the grey topper, the cut-away morning coat, the half-inch-striped trousers, the four-buttoned grey waistcoat, the starched collar, grey neckwear and, of course, the tightly wrapped, smartly packed black umbrella.

No one knows the historical significance behind each of these pieces of clothing. There is a story that the grey toppers can be traced back to early races at Ascot when people carried rabbits in their hats to the track. (Some say that before the horse evolved to its present shape, it looked like a big rabbit and, during the early years at Ascot, the only animals that raced were rabbits who chased grey-hound dogs around a circular track.)

But so much for history. One doesn't buy a cut-away suit in London, one hires it at Moss Bros. (pronounced Maws Braws). Moss Bros. is to the suit-hire business what Lloyd's is to the insurance business. From Ascot to Lord's to Eton to Harrow to the Royal Garden Parties and society weddings, Moss Bros. hire-suits are on parade.

When I went to Moss Bros. to hire mine, I found four-teen men in front of me. A straw poll revealed that most of us were for Ascot, though two admitted to the Eton-Harrow cricket match and one said the Royal Garden Party. The clerk who took care of me said that the suit he was letting me have had seen service at two horse shows, a Coronation, one Westminster baptism, a flower show at Sussex and a wedding which brought together two of Great Britain's leading families. The suit had never been to Ascot before, but the clerk was confident it would, like every Moss Bros. suit, do its duty. The cost for complete hire was £3 10s. per day.

The only question which presented itself was whether I should wear the backless waistcoat or not. The clerk said, "We never like to interfere in these matters, but the naked-shoulder-blade model is coming into its own and you would be perfectly correct in wearing it. I know this may sound rather daring, but at times one must be courageous."

It was one of those decisions one hates to make. I searched my conscience and finally decided to throw caution to the wind. I would wear the naked-shoulder-blade model in spite of everybody. When it comes to fashion I've always been known as a pace-setter.

After hiring the morning coat, the naked-shoulder-blade waistcoat and the striped trousers, I procured an umbrella and strode out to Hyde Park for a dress rehearsal. There I was shocked to discover that there are very few Englishmen who know anything about umbrellas. It happened this way. There was a dry spell of about five minutes during London's famed inclement weather and I was doing my best to roll up my umbrella when a dapper man wearing a derby, a starched collar and an old school tie stopped and said, "I beg your pardon. You seem to be a stranger here and, if you don't mind my saying so, you're making a muck-up of that umbrella."

I looked a little hurt.

"Oh, forgive me for not introducing myself. My name is Gerald Spokes and I'm a member of the Royal Umbrella and Parasol Society, an organization devoted to correcting the mishandling of umbrellas in the British Isles."

"The mishandling of umbrellas?"

"Yes. You see, most of the great umbrella men have died out and the art of sporting an umbrella is fast disappearing. Our society sends out voluntary members to give instructions—free of charge, of course—in order to correct these flagrant violations of proper umbrella taste and decency. Would you care to have some instruction?"

I said I'd be very happy to receive some.

"Good. Now the first thing you must learn is the nomenclature. There is the point at the bottom. Then there is the mainmast which runs up and meets the clutch, or handle. Just before the mainmast is the control button where you open or close the umbrella and there are the ribs and the pleated silk. Each piece of the umbrella plays its own important part, and without any one of them the whole instrument could easily sag or fall to pieces.

"Your umbrella is not badly built, though it is a little racy for this late in the afternoon. Malacca handles such as yours are preferred before four o'clock. But being an American, I don't imagine anyone will bother you about it.

"Now I noticed, while I was watching you before, that you twirled your umbrella. Sir, I can't impress upon you enough what bad taste this is. An occasional twirl in early morning is tolerated but never, never in the afternoon!

"You were also using your umbrella as a cane. Even if you had a bad limp, which you don't seem to have, it is against all decent propriety to use your umbrella as a cane. It must be carried with your gloves one inch from your body and draped over your left arm exactly six inches from the wrist bone, the open part of the handle or clutch facing in. And you must be careful that the umbrella does not swing more than ten degrees in any direction.

"So far so good. The next question is, what is an umbrella good for? The most important use for an umbrella is, of course, for hailing taxicabs. But there are so few of us who know how to hail a taxi in the correct manner. Let me show you.

"Stand with your feet about nine inches apart, firmly planted on the pavement. Take the umbrella from its left-arm circling position and bring it over across your chest. Then, in one motion, raise it so that the forearm is at a forty-five-degree angle to the body and that there is no daylight between the arm and the side of the body.

"Do not wave your arm and do not make a thrust at a taxi. You may flip some taxi-meters by mistake and there will be the devil to pay. The only time to extend your arm is when some bounder stations himself in front of you and tries to steal your cab. Then raise the umbrella, full length from the body, to ninety degrees and clout him over the head.

"The umbrella can also be used to acknowledge a greeting, but only with another man. You still have to tip your derby to a woman, and if you wave and tip at the same time you may trip yourself up.

"Another important use for the umbrella is for rapping on doors, which is far preferable to ringing a bell. In such cases you grip the umbrella in the centre at the balance point and, moving the wrist up and down, you rap rap

rap with the handle. If there is no answer you can always use the umbrella to open a transom and climb in that way.

"The umbrella has very important investigating properties and is particularly valuable in a park for poking paper lunch bags that might still have some food in them, and also for poking under rocks for fishing worms.

"I wish to point out one more thing. You never roll an umbrella when it's wet, and you always roll from the bottom up, making sure the ribs are locked and the silken pleats are equi-distant before you secure the button."

I thanked Mr. Spokes very much.

"Don't thank me; thank the Royal Umbrella and Parasol Society. And now, if you'll excuse me, I must hail a taxi."

Mr. Spokes crossed his right arm over, gripped the handle firmly and in one movement brought it across his chest smartly at a 45-degree angle. It was a beautiful manœuvre and there was no daylight showing between the arm and the side of the body.

After receiving this invaluable drill in proper umbrella usage, I went over to Fortnum and Mason, the food store, and ordered a hamper for the day. Tradition demands that during Royal Ascot you either eat in the Royal Enclosure, or at the White Club tent, or next to your car in the parking lot with a food hamper from Fortnum and Mason.

The clerk told me Royal Ascot called for lobster, chicken and tongue, potato salad, cheese, peaches and champagne. He told me the hamper should be placed about four feet from the rear door of the car and eaten at least forty-five minutes before the first race. The hamper cost me three pounds, including the bottle of champagne.

There was only one more matter to be attended to— the question of the Royal Enclosure. It seems that the place to be at Ascot is the Royal Enclosure, where the Queen and five hundred selected people are located. It is so exclusive that up to this year no divorced persons were allowed in the enclosure, even to get a glimpse of the horses. But this time I heard that the barriers had been let down and divorced persons were being allowed in. Although it was tough on my wife, I immediately went out and got a divorce. So there I was, dressed in a Moss Bros. cut-away suit with the naked-shoulder-blade waistcoat, provisioned by Fortnum and Mason and completely divorced from my wife, going hick lickety split to Ascot. Jamaica Racetrack was never like this.

Suddenly my Rolls-Royce stopped doing hick lickety split and went awr, mawr, gawr. Since Ascot Week is a royal week, under royal patronage, it wasn't surprising that I got into one of the most royal traffic jams of all time. The two-mile road from Windsor to Ascot was crowded with cars, bumper to bumper, and people, topper to topper. Everybody and His Lord High Chamberlain were off to the races, and it was only by a miracle that I managed to arrive in time for the first engagement. (It cost a quid to park, which shows you what kind of layout Ascot is.)

Taking my hamper in my right hand and my umbrella in the left hand I surged forth with the multitude.

Ascot is divided into many little islands of society. Besides the Royal Enclosure, there are the Paddock, where the horses mingle freely with the people; Tattersalls, where the bookmakers make book; the Silver Ring, where people known as the Ascot Snobs maintain boxes; the Heath, where the commoners stand; and a Crèche, complete with sand pit, where children play while their parents watch the tote boards.

I first tried to get into the Royal Enclosure, but I was rudely turned away. I produced my divorce papers and the deposit slip on my cut-away suit from Moss Bros., but the guards would not admit me. It seemed a shabby way to treat someone from across the seas.

I took my hamper to the paddock and started to spread my lunch on the grass. Someone with an Ascot Authority badge approached me. "I'm sorry, you can't picnic here. The grass is reserved for the horses."

"But," I protested, "I paid three quid and ten bob for this hamper and I'm hungry."

"Sorry, sir," he replied. "Hampers are not permitted. We provide food at the track. Why don't you go over to one of the refreshment stands and have some jellied eels?"

"Some jellied what?"

"Eels, sir. They're delicious. Now get along before we put you in the gaol."

"The what?"

"The gaol. That's where we put people who spread their hampers all over the nickety-nick grass."

Not wanting to go to the gaol, I packed up my hamper and went over to have some jellied eels. Jellied eels can be eaten with or without a pint. On my first try the eel started to drip (it was a hot day) and I caught the gravy in my grey topper. It was a mistake. A man in a cut-away suit approached me. He flashed a card. "I'm a Moss Bros. inspector. That's a very serious offence you have just committed. May I please see your deposit slip?"

I showed it to him and he wrote something on the back.

"Moss Bros. have ruled people off the course for far less than this. Since you are a foreigner we'll let you off with a warning. When eating jellied eels you let the gravy drip on to the grass."

I apologized and put the topper back on my head. The gravy ran down to my collar.

He took the deposit slip back again and wrote some more. "When one allows gravy to fall into one's grey topper, one does not put it back on the head again until it is emptied."

I took the tail of my morning coat and wiped off the gravy from my collar.

"No, no, no," he screamed in despair. "The tail of the coat is never used as a napkin."

I handed over the deposit slip.

"Now get on with you and mind your manners or I'll take the suit away from you right here on the track."

I walked away quickly before he found something else wrong.

The horses were in the paddock and everyone was jammed together looking at them. Unfortunately I had my umbrella in the ring and tripped one of the horses. A man from the Umbrella Authority grabbed me by the arm. "One does not use one's umbrella to trip the horses. One keep's one's umbrella on one's arm or leans on it at parade rest behind the right hip. If you don't know how to use an umbrella properly we'll see that you are forbidden ever to use it again."

The horse got up from the ground and I wiped off his flank with the tail of my tailcoat. When I looked up the inspector from Moss Bros. was standing right beside me.

Abashed by his watchful presence, I left the paddock with the still full Fortnum and Mason hamper. My collar had wilted a little from the heat and the jellied-eel gravy, but otherwise I was perfectly attired. I made once again for the Royal Enclosure, which had now filled up with flowered frocks, cut-away suits and black umbrellas. Just as I was approaching it, the same Moss Bros. inspector caught up with me and whispered through his teeth, "Straighten your topper, pull up your cravat, button up your waistcoat and look smart. Where do you think you are—at a Henley Boat Race?"

I straightened up, but he continued to lecture me. "Look at all those Moss Bros. cut-aways out there. You don't see one topper out of line, and look at you. Even the stripes on your trousers are crooked. Now go about your business and be careful, or else it's back to the Strand for you."

Seeing a large crowd of spectators and Her Majesty walking in the midst of them, I wormed my way through the Royal Enclosure fence and waited patiently for somebody to introduce me. But when Her Majesty walked by, she looked the other way. One of the bystanders, seeing the tears in my eyes, said, "The Queen Mother and Princess Margaret are meeting people over in that crowd. Perhaps you will be presented to them". I rushed over, fought my way through, tearing my coat on a maharaja's diamond pin, and stood hopefully facing the Queen Mother and Princess Margaret. They walked right by.

"Try the Duke of Edinburgh," a man suggested. I ran over, pushed through a large gathering of ladies, and, waving my umbrella at the Duke, I smiled hopefully. The ladies were furious and pushed me back out of sight, tearing my waistcoat in the bargain.

As I got up from the ground, someone else said: "The Duchess of Kent and Princess Alexandra are over there." It was too late. They had already disappeared into the Royal Box.

I took my hamper to the edge of the field and spread it out to eat. The man from Moss Bros. jumped out from behind a tree. "There you are. Everyone has been talking about you. Look at you. Your coat is torn, your naked-shoulder-blade waistcoat is askew, you're missing your collar button. I've had enough. Give me the suit."

"Right here on the field?"

"You can go out the back gate. No one will see you."

I took off the coat, the waistcoat, the shirt, the tie and the pants. "Can I keep the topper until tomorrow, in case it rains?" I asked.

"All right, but you better wear it correctly."

I escaped out through the back gate before anybody

could spot me. It was a fine Royal Ascot, even though I didn't meet anyone worth mentioning and they took away the suit. But it needed a cleaning, anyway.

THE BARBARIANS OF HIALEAH

THE LACK OF tradition at Hialeah is very disappointing to someone who was almost presented to the Queen at Ascot. Although the racetrack is probably one of the most beautiful in the world, the attire worn by the people in attendance leaves much to be desired. We who have worn the topper, the swallowtail and the striped pants, we who have tripped through the Royal Enclosure—usually on someone else's umbrella—find it regrettable that Floridians have no interest in anything but the horses.

The only concession they'll make to clothes is that people who sit in the grandstands will wear bright coloured shirts, those who sit in the reserved clubhouse seats will wear checkered shirts and those who sit in the boxes will wear ties and coats.

Many things have shocked me about Hialeah. One is the behaviour of the crowd. At Ascot we don't feel it's proper to urge the horses on to victory. We believe an English horse will always do his best and requires no encouragement from the spectators.

But at Hialeah I found the audience shouting at the horses throughout the race, and making remarks about the animals that I hope never reached their ears.

Another major difference I found between the two tracks was Americans always want the horse they bet on to win, while we in England, although we also bet, are more interested in knowing if the horses have had a good time.

D

There are a few things that Hialeah has that Ascot has not. For one thing, they have Seminole Indians parading around in full dress. You can look from one end of Ascot to the other and you won't find a Seminole Indian.

Hialeah also has flamingos—an estimated 350 of them. The only thing that Ascot has comparable to them are jellied eels. The one disadvantage is that you can't eat the flamingos, while a jellied eel is an Ascot duffer's chief form of nourishment.

At the Florida track you can see the entire race from start to finish, which forces the spectator to concentrate. At Ascot, if you see the horses finish one race you are considered ahead for the day.

Hialeah has a distinct dislike for bookies. Almost all the money bet there goes through the pari-mutuel machines. If a bookie is caught at the track he is taken by the scruff of the neck and the seat of the pants and asked politely to leave. At Ascot the bookie is the most revered man on the track, loved as much by the people as he is by the horses. English bookies are given special stands to operate from and you have your choice of odds from over one hundred cheerful, money-waving men. It is a form of free enterprise that has been dying out in America, where automation has even reached into the sport of kings.

American horses are treated as prima donnas. They have heated stalls, formula foods and cashmere blankets.

We in England don't believe in spoiling our animals. We give them oats and Guinness Stout and let them rough it in the stables. It gives the horses more of a sense of responsibility, and there is no desire on the part of our horses to get back to their stalls as there is at Hialeah.

There is one other difference worth mentioning. Americans use an electric starting gate to make sure all the horses will leave at the same time. At Ascot we prefer the free start. If a horse does not want to run that day, and many of them have indicated they didn't, he is free to stay at the start for the entire race, and the next day, too, if he so desires.

Hialeah has many innovations we lack at Ascot, including a hairdresser for women on the premises, electric tote boards, comfortable chairs, simple programmes and an excellent loud-speaker system. But at the same time we at Ascot have tradition behind us. When our horses glance into the stands and gaze at that sea of toppers and pearl-buttoned waistcoats, you can see pride in their stride and you can hear them saying, "Thank God, I race in England."

ARE YOU SURE IT'S CRICKET?

One of the most thrilling experiences you can have in Europe is attending the Eton-Harrow cricket match at Lord's. As everyone knows, Eton and Harrow are public schools, which means in England that they are private, and there is such a tradition of rivalry between them that a spectator has to be very careful while sitting in the stands—the person sitting next to him may be wearing the other school's necktie.

Although it was my first cricket match, I certainly enjoyed it. The thing that struck me most about the Harrow-Eton contest was how similar cricket is to our national game of baseball. It was almost as if I were watching the Brooklyn Dodgers and the New York Giants having a go of it at Ebbets Field. How many times have Americans said, "The Battle of the Alamo was won on the playing field of Ebbets?"

Let's not talk about the differences, but about the similarities between cricket and baseball. First, we were amazed how the spectators at Lord's resembled the ones you see at the Brooklyn matches. Nearly all the men were wearing morning coats and grey top hats with waistcoats, and they all carried umbrellas. The women were splendidly outfitted in large straw hats and lovely flowered dresses. The men wore flowers in their lapels designating which team they were rooting for, a custom, no doubt, which they picked up from our own baseball games at home.

While cricket differs from baseball in a few ways, the spirit in which the game is played is very similar. Etonians and Harrovians are not so much interested in the result as they are in how the match is played. Was it a clean win? Did both sides have fun? Did the team make new friends out of the contest and did everyone hit and field as hard as the circumstances permitted? And so it is with Dodgerovians and Giantonians. As Mr. Leo Durocher, the ex-strategist of the New York team, pointed out many times, "It isn't who wins, but how you play the game that counts."

As in baseball, a cricket team must be spurred and booted and on the field at least ten minutes before the umpires go out. The visiting team is met and welcomed with the utmost consideration by the local captain and his team. Cricketers, like baseballers, realize their respective sports are not so much to win cups, pennants or glory as to meet men like themselves who wish to spend a relaxing day on the green, hitting and fielding the elusive red ball.

Instead of pitchers, cricket features bowlers, and instead of hitters, cricket has batsmen. But the object in both games is to hit the ball as hard as you possibly can in order to score as many runs for your team as is humanly possible. In cricket the score gets a little high sometimes, going as high as nine hundred runs a game, but when you consider that one cricket game can take two days or a test match five days, the number of runs scored doesn't seem unreasonable.

Cricket players always break for lunch and have a ten-minute recess for tea. The tea interval was undoubtedly adopted from America's seventh-inning stretch.

As in our national sport, the spectators of cricket applaud politely when someone has made a good batting or fielding play but refrain from mentioning it if anyone has the misfortune to make an error or strike out. Only on rare occasions may the spectators raise their voices. When a man scores a century, which means he has made one hundred runs and is a sort of a Willie Mays, "three cheers for the occasion" are perfectly in order.

In discussing the similarities between the games one cannot overlook how the umpires resemble each other. A cricket umpire, like a baseball umpire, is the most respected man on the field and his eyesight and honesty are unquestioned by the spectators. It is this faith in umpires which probably makes both sports so popular with the players as well as the people in the stands.

Anyway, to get back to the Harrow-Eton match, it was a sitter for Harrow, which scored a decisive victory this year by nine wickets. For a while it looked as if Eton might win the day, and how they blew it is something I'll never know.

Ever since I attended my first Eton-Harrow match, I've been an enthusiastic American fan of British sport. Not long ago I hied myself over to Eton on St. Andrew's Day to witness the 115th playing of the famous Wall Game. I suspect that there are one or two readers who don't know what the Wall Game is, but are too embarrassed to admit it. There is really no need to be embarrassed, because some old Etonians who have been playing it for 115 years still don't understand the game.

The Wall Game is one of the unique athletic contests

in the world. For one thing, the only place it is played is Eton; for another, no one has scored a goal in a St. Andrew's Day match in forty years; and for a third, it is one of the few sports where it is impossible for the spectator to see what is going on.

When I arrived on the playing field of Eton, a crowd had already gathered. St. Andrew's Day is also Parent's Day at the famed public school, and Etonians dressed in starched collars and striped pants stood with their parents in mud up to their tailcoats waiting for the contest to begin.

There were mud and fog everywhere, perfect Wall Game weather, I was told. One old-timer complained it was the cleanest day he had ever seen. Through the fog I saw the famous wall. At one end of the 110-yard field was a tree, which was the goal known as Bad Calx, and at the other end of the field was the goal of Good Calx, which happened to be a door leading into the masters' garden.

The St. Andrew's Day Wall Game is played between two teams, one made up of the Collegers (The Brains), students who are at Eton on scholarship, and the other the Oppidans (The Brawn), made up of students who pay.

There are ten players on each side. Besides the wall, the most important prop is the football. The object of the game, it was explained to me, was to push the ball along the wall until you reached a certain place in Calx, where you could then attempt to score a shy. A shy is not a goal, but since goals are so rarely scored the shy is the next best thing, and the scoring of one is enough to win the game. Are you still with me?

Both teams gather against the wall in a huddle called a "bully." They look like they're trying to push the wall down, but it's just a spectator's illusion. The lad next to me, who was trying to help, said, "It's just like

American football, you know, where the team goes into a huddle—the only difference being in the Wall Game they never come out of the huddle until the game is over."

The only similarity to American football is that the players are allowed to knuckle and gouge each other and bash their heads against the wall or the ground. Since the whole thing is played in mud, usually away from the prying eyes of the referee, practically anything goes in a bully, except that you can't sit on the ball. You can kneel on it, though. (The greatest hero in the history of the Wall Game was J. K. Stephens, who, in 1877, knelt on the ball for twenty-five minutes in Bad Calx, a record which has never been equalled.)

The game lasts for an hour. A gain of twelve inches in either direction is considered an extraordinary feat comparable to ex-King Farouk running a four-minute mile. The only time the bully breaks up is if one of the players finds his face has been pushed down more than three feet in the mud. If this happens he may call for air and the players have to separate.

The lad next to me said half apologetically, "I know it's difficult for you people from across the Pond to get enthused about the Wall Game but it's a very special game played by very special people. Sometimes you don't see the ball for five years. It's quite usual to see nothing. But it's much easier on the mothers that way."

I watched as a cloud of steam rose from the bully. Suddenly, after forty-five minutes, the ball slipped out of the middle and someone kicked it.

"I saw the ball," I shouted excitedly. "Look, there it is!"

"Yes, you're quite lucky," he said. "I've never seen such an open game."

For the record, the Collegers beat the Oppidans by a score of one shy to nil, their first win since 1949.

I have been asked many times since if the Wall Game is worth seeing. The answer is yes. Until you've seen it, you can't get any idea of what the Battle of Waterloo was all about.

AUTO POLO IN PARIS

ONE DAY I thought I'd go over and call on Mr. Milton Wallach, an intrepid American who was living on the Right Bank before moving to the American Hospital. If you have never heard of him, he is the man who has been trying to stir up international interest in the French game of auto polo, which is now played every day on the winding streets and majestic avenues of Paris.

"I know something of the game," he told me. "For example, I know that hitting a pedestrian counts one point for each adult, a half point for each child and two points if the victim is a tourist. What I would like to know is, can I be credited with a score if my car is in reverse gear? Last week I backed into a bus and the referee waved his baton and said I was offside."

Mr. Wallach was of the opinion that Paris cars should be marked with the ratings of the driver. It is unfair, he pointed out, to pit a ten-crash car against one which has only scraped a fender. The two best playing fields in Paris for auto polo, he thought, are the Place de la Concorde and the Etoile.

The Sunday before he had achieved his best score since he'd been in Paris. "Zooming into play around the Etoile, I scored a carom shot. This involved blocking a Renault 4 CV against a Simca Aronde and then hitting two motorcyclists in such a way as to drive them into the air feet first. I'm a modest man when it comes to auto polo, but when I heard the cheers from the sidelines I'll have to admit my head swam."

In playing the game Mr. Wallach told me that he had experimented with many different kinds of mounts, but had come to the conclusion that a Ford Country Sedan was the best. "Testing it against city play, I found it responded very well and that with power steering I tired very little after several chukkers on the boulevards. My mistake was thinking that because I had achieved success in Paris I was ready for the Route Nationale.

"While perhaps it's unfair to complain about the infractions of the rules from the relative safety of a bed at the American Hospital, I do feel that clipping should not be permitted unless both offenders approach from the same direction. Just as soon as I can obtain a new motor and body from Michigan, I expect to return to the field of play and meanwhile would appreciate anything you can do to generate interest among other visitors who may wish to form an auto-polo club in Paris. I think only eight-crash ratings should be admitted."

He believed that the insurance companies are trying to discourage the game, but he said: "I do feel it will eventually prove the answer to the tremendous over production of motor-cars."

On hearing of my interest in the game, Mr. William Schwarz, the secretary of the French Auto Polo Association, wrote several days later to me to inform me that new rules of scoring had been added in the last few years.

The new rules state that French drivers are scored according to the following:

1. Accidentally hitting a pedestrian when no previously established motive can be proven . . . one point.

2. Planning a concerted attack upon a pedestrian and seeing it through to its eventual accomplishment . . . two points.

3. Singling out a specific pedestrian from among a large

crowd crossing at an intersection, attacking the single pedestrian without touching the others . . . three points.

4. Pregnant women or a woman carrying a child under three years of age . . . four points.

5. Male or female tourist snapping pictures in the middle of the Avenue de la Grande-Armée or the Etoile, if hit from behind . . . five points; or straight on . . . six points.

There is currently an amendment pending concerning school children. Many French drivers consider that the point value of six for school children is too low. They claim they are often forced to chase the children and have frequent misses due to the children's nimbleness. Several members have asked that the point value be raised to seven. A compromise may be reached by giving six points for hitting a child and an extra point if he's on a bicycle.

In scoring, the French Auto Polo Association requires the signatures of two witnesses, neither of whom is related to the driver.

But auto polo is not the first game that has been played with cars in Paris. For many years the French have been playing something called auto soccer. The sport, which originated at the Place de la République and spread all the way over to the Porte de St. Cloud, requires the participants to hit a pedestrian and then try to push him into the other fellow's goal. Only the tyres may be used in pushing the pedestrian toward the goal once he has been hit. Passing is permitted from one car to the other. The goalkeepers, who are Paris policemen, are the only ones who can touch the pedestrian (the ball) with their hands.

The scoring is similar to auto polo except for the penalties. If the opposing car passes a red light, then the other team has a "free throw"—the pedestrian is placed in the *clous*, or pedestrian walk, and the car, with a two-hundred-yard advantage, is allowed to hit him without interference from the opposition.

Some auto-soccer players have tried to use motor-scooter drivers instead of pedestrians, but the results have not been as good. Although the "ball" is livelier, there is too much chance of the motor-scooterist getting caught in the spokes of the car, which slows up the game no end.

THE PARKER PEN APPROACH

ONE OF THE main differences between Rome and Paris is in the merchandise peddled by the street merchants of Rome. In Paris when a man sidles up to you on the street he either wants to change your money or sell you dirty postcards, leather wallets, Moroccan rugs, hot diamonds or an evening of Pigalle sin.

But the Roman sidewalk merchants, as far as I could tell, deal in only two products—hand-carved cameos and Parker pens. It's understandable that these fellows could create an interest in cameos, but why they should think Americans are queer for Parker pens is something I could never figure out.

One morning as I left the Excelsior Hotel a Parker pen man came up to me and took one of the instruments out of the deep recesses of his pocket. "Hot Parker pen right off the boat," he said. "Best pen in the world. Hot pen. Seven bucks, okay?"

When I shook my head he came down to five and then in a last desperate bid he said, "Two fifty. I lose money, but I like Americans, Okay?"

I bought the pen and then invited my friend, Angelo, for a cup of *espresso*.

"Tell me, Angelo, where do these pens really come from?"

"Hot off ship like I said."

I slipped him two thousand lire. "The truth, Angelo. I'm not a policeman, but I must have the truth. I want to go into your business."

Angelo gripped the two thousand lire and said, "Okay, I tell you. They're made in Torino at a factory."

"Then they're not Parker pens, as you and your friends advertise?"

"Sure they Parker pens. They say Parker pens right on them. So if they say it they're Parker pens."

"But it also says on the pen that they're made in the U.S.A. That part isn't true, is it?"

"No, like I said, they're made in Torino. They just put the U.S.A. on them so people will think they're made in the U.S.A., so people will think they're hot pens, right off the boat."

"And the real Parker pen people have nothing to do with the Torino company?"

"Of course not. Why should they if they're made in Torino?"

"Angelo, tell me honestly, how long will these pens write?"

Angelo thought about this for a moment. "Sometimes twenty-four hours, but one never knows. One time fellow brought me pen back and said it only wrote for two hours. His hand was all covered with ink. The trouble was bottom part is made of hard wax and if you get it hot the wax melts and the ink spills all out. I told him he shouldn't hold it in his hand so the wax will melt. He got mad so I go away fast."

I asked Angelo if he would take me to the place in Rome where all the merchants bought the pens. He refused, so I slipped him another thousand lire and he agreed.

Angelo took me to the old Ghetto Quarter of Rome and after winding through several narrow streets we came to a little store without a sign over it.

We went in and my mouth started to water. I've never seen so many Parker pens in my life. The man was suspicious until Angelo explained the mission. He then proudly showed me the stock. Besides Parker pens he also had thousands of Eversharps, also made in Torino. I guessed the total writing time of all the pens in the shop to be at least sixty days.

I bought a dozen, at equivalent in lire of sixty-five cents each, to give friends in Paris and also because Father's Day wasn't far away.

Angelo bought six more. On the way back he warned me not to sell any of the pens on the sidewalk in front of the Excelsior. "If you want, go over by the Colosseum and you'll get all the bus loads from American Express and Thomas Cook. But keep the pens in a cool place so the wax won't melt. If anyone asks you where you got them, tell them 'Hot off boat.' Americans like that. They'll buy anything as long as it's hot off boat."

THE MOST EXPENSIVE CUP OF COFFEE IN THE WORLD

THE MOST interesting thing in Istanbul for a globe-trotting tourist is the famed covered bazaar, an area of about twelve city blocks containing two thousand shops selling everything from a ring which once belonged to Caesar to a backscratcher once used by a sultan's wife who had poison ivy. The bazaar, which dates back to the sixteenth century, is populated by the shrewdest merchants on the globe and there has never been a deal consummated, to their knowledge, where the customer came out on top.

When the news had spread that a group of wealthy Americans had arrived to participate in the opening of the Istanbul Hilton there were celebrations in the bazaar all night. Manufacturers of bona fide antique jewellery went on three shifts, turning out sixteenth-, seventeenth- and eighteenth-century pieces. Signs were put up in all the shops: WELCOME, CONRAD HILTON. They were ready for us as they had never been ready for anyone in the bazaar's five-hundred-year history.

I went to the bazaar looking for a shop called Davud's, recommended to me by Tex and Jinx. (Tex and Jinx Bensika, that is; some very old Turkish friends of mine.) As I entered the bazaar several merchants approached me with friendly smiles and open arms.

I asked them if they knew where Davud's shop was.

"What a shame," said one of them. "Davud died last week. Please come into my shop. It's much cooler in there."

"Davud," said another of the merchants, "is on vacation. He went to Ankara for a month. He told me to look after his customers."

"Davud," said a third, "went bankrupt. I bought all his things. Please, mister, this way."

I fought them off and kept walking through the bazaar.

In one shop I saw Abel Green, the editor of *Variety*, looking at an antique vase. I stopped in to hear the dialogue.

The merchant holding the vase said, "There are only two like it in the world. The other one is in the Metropolitan Museum of Art in New York."

"How much is it?" asked Mr. Green.

"For you I'll make a special price. Five hundred dollars."

"Why, you robber," said Mr. Green, "the Metropolitan Museum of Art is only asking $450 for theirs."

I went on asking for Davud, but to no avail. Davud, I was told, had just drowned in the Bosphorus; he had been arrested for drunken driving; he was emigrating to America; his shop had burned down; his wife was having a baby; he had just been appointed Ambassador to Yemen. No one was talking.

Finally I stopped to admire a ring in a window. It was my mistake. Before I knew it I was pulled into the shop and seated on a stool.

The merchants of the Istanbul bazaar hate to discuss business. The first thing they ask you is, "Would you like a cup of Turkish coffee?"

I said I would. This could turn out to be the most expensive cup of coffee in the world. It could cost someone up to $10,000 before he got out of the shop. While waiting for the coffee, the man started out on his jewellery. Every piece had a history behind it. One belonged to an unfaithful wife of a sultan who had had her head chopped off for stepping on the sultan's toe. A ring had belonged to Constantine, a pillbox was once owned by Cleopatra.

I said I wasn't interested.

"What about a nice Turkish wedding ring for your wife? Nicky Hilton bought one for Terry Moore yesterday. I have only one other left." He reached into the safe and brought out a ring of diamonds, sapphires and emeralds mounted on five gold bands.

"Hilton only had four gold bands on his," the merchant said.

"Why didn't you sell him this one?"

"I was saving it for you."

The haggling began. He asked $250. I laughed at him. He began to cry. "No one has ever questioned my prices before. Please don't humiliate me like this. Pay what I ask you."

I laughed some more. He cried louder. "There are only two like it in the world. Two hundred and thirty dollars. Two hundred. All right, I'll lose my shirt, $180. Please, you're killing me, $150. My last price. If they hear about this in the bazaar, I'm through. Don't look at me like that. I'll make it $130. Please—$130 and I'll throw in a second cup of coffee."

I had the second cup of coffee and walked out with the ring. Across the way a jeweller called me. "Psst! I've got to talk to you. What did he sell you?"

"A ring," I whispered. "Why, isn't he a reputable jeweller?"

"Of course he's reputable. You know, his brother owns a glass factory in town, but I'm sure there is no connection."

It was my turn to cry.

"If I had gone to Davud's," I said, "this would never have happened."

"Davud," the jeweller said, "that's my name. Come in, sit down, have a cup of coffee. Now, this harem ring which Napoleon gave to Josephine . . ."

BREAKING THE ICE AT ST. MORITZ

EVERY YEAR millions of civilized people, young and old, tall and short, rich and poor, gather on the snowy slopes of their favourite country to engage in a perilous sport called skiing. The sport, which dates back to Time Immemorial (Time Immemorial was a little town just outside of Copenhagen), is attracting more and more enthusiasts each year, tempting them with cool breezes, breathtaking speeds, ticklish thrills and self-satisfying broken legs. The mould out of which good skiers are cast is usually made of plaster of Paris, and should be placed between the knee and the ankle, depending on the seriousness of the injury. There are some people who say skiing accidents are unavoidable, and it's true. But before the accident comes, before the enthusiast finds his leg hanging from a hospital pulley, I believe he can get more out of the sport than he's getting now. Having won the uphill slalom at St. Moritz, and a fox-trot contest at Zermatt, I feel I am in a position to advise the fledgling as well as the expert on this sport of sports, this maker of men, this waylayer of women, this child of nature which we call skiing.

Winter sports being what they are, and winter-sports enthusiasts being what they are, it's very hard for a person who doesn't ski to turn up at a ski resort. On the other hand, statistics prove that for every person who comes to a resort to ski, there are two and three-quarter persons who don't. (The other fraction represents a person who gives no quarter.) What do these people do? Where can they turn? What is their future?

In St. Moritz, the heart of the broken-limb country, where a man must prove himself first on skis and then on a stretcher, I found the answer. This resort has made it easy on non-skiers. In place of skiing you can go down on the bobsled or the Cresta—one on the seat of your pants and the other on the flat of your stomach. By reaching speeds of sixty or seventy miles an hour, you get the same feeling as if you were on skis, and instead of running the risk of breaking your leg, the only thing you can possibly break on the bobsled or Cresta is your neck.

But for those who, like me, want the glory without the danger, there are ways of getting around doing anything. If you follow instructions, the only risk you'll take is burning your tongue on the hot chocolate which everyone drinks at a ski resort when the long day is over.

It's all a question of looking good. The first place to look good is on the ski train. When leaving for a ski resort the non-skier should be completely dressed in ski pants, ski boots and goggles. The non-skier must remember that clothes make the skier, the skier doesn't make the clothes

You don't have to carry any skis, but you should have two ski sticks with you. If you want to look good before the train starts, you can practice low crouches, jump turns, parallel swings, Christiania stems on the train platform. This will impress everyone on the station and you'll be a legend before you even get on the train.

Once aboard you can either wax your ski sticks or study snow bulletins. It's all right to strike up conversations about skiing with other passengers provided they are not going to the same resort. When walking to the dining car you can either use the "alternate step" or you can do "stakning." The alternate step needs no explanation—you just put one foot after another. But stakning is more difficult. You have to keep your feet parallel and close together and slide along with the help of your ski sticks. This is very difficult to do without skis, but if the non-skier waxes the bottoms of his ski boots he'll get a nice effect.

When he arrives at the ski resort the non-skier has to be very careful. If there is snow on the ground he may be in trouble. One method of solving the problem would be to jump off the train from the top step and then scream, "My ankle, my ankle, I think I broke it!"

As soon as you reach the hotel, strap up one of your ankles with adhesive tape and for the rest of the time limp around. You never have to explain at a ski resort why you're limping. It's taken for granted, and you can even get people to buy you free drinks if you look as if you're in enough pain.

Once you're free of skiing you can stay up all night, drinking and having a ball, and sleep in the daytime. If you feel up to it, you can also collect ski medals in your spare afternoons.

Most ski medals can be bought in souvenir shops and others can be picked up accidentally. I was sitting in the lobby of the Palace Hotel one afternoon when Andreas

Badrutt, the owner, walked by. He gave me a medal for skiing down Piz Nair, one of the highest and most frightening ski slopes in Switzerland. Another time I had lunch at the Corviglia Club, and while I was ordering a dozen snails and a bottle of Rhine wine someone sewed the club's insignia on my ski jacket. It's these little things that make skiing fun for non-skiers.

A person may raise the question of boredom. "If I don't ski, won't I be bored?" The answer is no. Ski resorts have ping-pong tables, bowling alleys, juke boxes and deck chairs. They also have beautiful women. Most beautiful women don't like to go skiing because they're afraid of breaking their beautiful legs. This leaves unlimited possibilities for the non-skier. Although women admire the athletic prowess of a skiing man, there is an old St. Moritz saying that "A bird in the lobby of a hotel is worth two on a ski lift." For some reason the saying holds true all over the world.

For those who are not content with bending over the bar and are bent on hitting the slope (it usually hits back), here are some idle remarks about the sport. Skiing is the method of gliding on snow with the aid of two pieces of wood (or aluminium) fastened to the feet. By manipulating these pieces of wood, the skier can steer himself between rocks, trees and over other skiers. The expression "over my dead body" originally was used by someone who had just had a skiing spill. Later it was adopted by Mr. Casey Stengel of baseball fame, and he used the expression so many times that it has now become common usage in the English language.

There is no one too young or too old to engage in skiing. In some Scandinavian countries three-month-old babies are tied to the tops of cigar boxes and shoved down mountains before they are able to talk. In Switzerland, wheel chairs are equipped with skis and old men and women are encouraged to compete in jumping contests in wheel chairs.

In discussing the art of skiing let us take up some of the things that are required of one who wishes to participate in the sport. The first thing, of course, is equipment. Without the right equipment the skier is immediately handicapped if not ostracized by everyone in the sporting world.

The main items of clothing necessary are—a pair of peg-top trousers which are worn inside the boot. As far as socks go there are two schools of thought on the subject. One school believes you should wear your socks *outside* the boot. It makes a much better colour combination for that part of the leg where colour is always needed. The other school thinks it's better to wear the sock *inside* the boot and also believes that the trouser should be held in place by an elastic band. I am a member of the first school (Class of '48). Since most skiers are going to spend more time in bars and hotel lobbies than they are on the ski course, appearance counts much more than safety, and a pair of bright woollen socks over well-polished boots can make all the difference in the world in the fast-moving social circles that skiing has become so much a part of.

Boots should be chosen with a great deal of care. They should have rubber soles so you can't slip on dance floors and enough room in them to store a sandwich or two in case you get hungry during the day. Many people make the mistake of buying boots that fit. When the inevitable accident occurs the boot then has to be cut off the swollen foot and a good fifteen or twenty bucks is thrown down the drain. If the farsighted skier purchases ski boots several sizes too big, he will not have to have the ski boot cut off his foot and he will be able to continue skiing even if the foot swells up to twice its normal size. This is worth keeping in mind.

The next item of clothing to be considered is the ski sweater. The best ski sweaters should have elks on them. Men should purchase sweaters with one large elk, and women, sweaters with two little elks looking at each other over a great divide. The elks should be alert and their horns should protrude up towards the neck. Incidentally, turtle necks may be warmer, but at the moment they're out of fashion and a good skier would cut his throat before being caught with one on.

Gloves should also have elks on them. The faces of the elks should face inward and their horns should be part of the finger design. In the case of mittens the elks do not necessarily have to face each other.

Goggles and ear muffs are optional. If you're going skiing with your wife the ear muffs are not optional but a necessity. Sun glasses should be worn at all times, as they make the rankest amateur skier look like the rankest professional.

That's all the equipment one needs, except if one wants to carry a pistol. The law about shooting skiers with broken legs has never been clearly defined. In the only case that has ever come to court, Oscar Heppleworth was acquitted of shooting his wife with his famous defence line, "They shoot horses, don't they?"

Now the question of choosing skis comes up. The length of the ski depends on the height of the person. A ski should reach the palm of the skier's hand just touching the nose of the embroidered elk. Longer skis are too difficult to manipulate and much heavier to carry on one's shoulder. Their only advantage is that you can clear a very large path for yourself when climbing with them up the hill.

Hickory and ash are the two best woods that skis are made of. Hickory, a nut-bearing tree, is solid, thick and hard grained, and its elasticity and pliability have been tested time and time again in schoolrooms all over the world. Ash is the most suitable wood that grows in Europe. It is not as good as hickory, but it's better than plywood, which is something in its favour.

The wood used for making skis should not contain knots. If your ski contains a knot, do "not" buy it. Once you have chosen the ski, then you must choose the binding. The binding should be strong enough to hold the shoe in place and at the same time flexible enough in case you want to leave the ski suddenly.

Ski sticks should be about six inches above the waist line and made of metal. They can be used to prevent you from falling and for roasting marshmallows in front of an open fireplace.

Having dealt with the question of equipment we are now faced with the problem of how to ski.

The best way of learning to ski is to hire an instructor. A ski instructor is probably the most patient man in the world and since he gets paid by the hour he doesn't care how much time you spend in the snow. The favourite phrase of the ski instructor is "If you fall you have to get up yourself. It's the only way you'll learn." If it looks as though you can't make it in a reasonable length of time, the instructor will bring you food and water, and a blanket if night is falling. But under no condition will he help you to get on your feet. If you don't suffer from frostbite, this is a lesson you'll remember for the rest of your skiing life.

The first thing every skier must master is the "involuntary fall." This means to be able to fall when you don't want to. It usually takes about five minutes to learn this, and once you have it down pat you can fall anywhere in the snow without the help of the instructor. Having learned the rudiments of falling, one should then try to pick up a few of the rudiments of staying up on the skis.

The easiest way to start off is to sit on the skis facing

forward. In this way you can always grab on to the shoe-laces of one of the better skiers if you feel you're getting into trouble.

When you feel you've built up confidence in a sitting position, try kneeling. The bindings on your knees may at first bother you but after a while you will get used to them. In the kneeling position you can always grab on to someone's leg if you lose control of yourself.

After you have mastered the kneeling position, you are then in line to try the run standing up. When you are in position, throw your arms tightly around the neck of the ski instructor, who should have his back toward you. Then give him a slight push. Both of you will go tumbling down the hill and for the first time you'll feel the thrill that comes to all skiers who have conquered one of God's most fearful elements—snow.

If your ski instructor becomes angry, fire him on the spot. Don't take any back talk from him, and remind him there are a lot of ski instructors who would be happy to earn the money he's earning, and could do a much better job of teaching you how to ski. This should end the argument on the spot. If not, you have two ski poles and by now you'll know what to do with them.

Following your first ride down the hill standing up you are now ready to practise some of the more intricate turns. The stem Christiania, the snow plough and the jump turn are all easy to learn and should not take more than five years with daily practice.

After learning the turns you can then go in for jumping. Keep your feet together when jumping and your crouch low. The sticks shouldn't be placed too near the feet, and the hands and arms should be at shoulder level. Jump for-ward and not straight up into the air. Keep your knees on your chest, your heels up and your toes down, and what-ever else you do, let your knees absorb the shock.

And above all, watch out for avalanches. An avalanche

can always spoil a good jump. If you jump into an avalanche, find a shelter quick. That's all there is to jumping. From here on out you're on your own.

Before signing off this instructive article on skiing, I'd like to add a list of don'ts that the skier must pay attention to if he expects to be well informed on the sport.

First, don't admit to people in bars that you are an amateur and have never skied before. If you're dressed properly you can look as good as the next fellow, and if you buy the drinks they'll believe anything you tell them.

Secondly, don't use bad language when you fall. If you must be profane, be profane towards the ski instructor and not towards the skis.

Don't ski near children. They will in all probability only laugh at you.

If you are a woman, do not wear sweaters that will cause other skiers to forget where they're going.

Don't try to stop yourself by crashing into a tree. It may be somebody's mother.

Don't spend more than $3,000 for your first ski outfit.

Don't flirt with girls in your ski class. You may wind up paying for their lessons.

Don't eat at the ski club. It's very expensive and when they find out you are not a member they'll throw you out in the snow.

Don't shoot polar bears from a moving ski lift. It's considered poor sportsmanship, even for beginners.

Well, it looks as if I've covered the subject pretty well and there isn't any more advice I can give. From now on it's up to each individual to get out there and join the winter madness. Remember, class, for each pair of skis on a snowy hill there is a pair of crutches waiting for you at the local hospital. The question is, how soon will you earn yours?

I was sitting in the lobby of the Palace Hotel sipping

tea and chewing on an old ski boot when I was approached by a large, good-looking man who introduced himself as Serge Oestesky. Serge asked if I liked skiing, and I said I didn't because it was too much work.

"I thought so," he said. "Let me introduce you to a sport that requires no work at all. All you have to do is lie on a sled and go down a hill called the Cresta. There are no ski-lift fees to pay, no chance of falling into the snow and no ski instructors to scream that you're doing everything wrong."

"It sounds interesting," I said, "but everyone says it's very dangerous. There are vicious rumours that a man can do eighty-five miles an hour on the course. People say that you can get killed on the run. They say you're not a skeleton rider unless you've broken at least one leg or both arms."

"Poppycock," said Serge. "Come down tomorrow morning and we'll fix you up. You'll never regret it." As an incentive he added, "Gregory Peck is going down to-morrow—probably right after you."

That sold me, and the next morning I showed up at nine o'clock. Serge took me into a nice warm hut and started throwing things at me. First he threw some thick knee pads, then elbow pads, then a pair of boots with steel rakes jutting out of the toes. When I put those on he gave me a football helmet and two metal shields for my hands. I started to break into a sweat.

"W-w-w-where's Gr-gr-gregory P-p-p-peck?" I asked Serge.

"Don't worry, he's coming," Serge said. "Come on down the run. I'll show you the skeleton."

"Th-th-the wh-wh-wh-what?"

"Skeleton. That's the sled. It's made of two rigid round steel runners which are welded to steel braces and a steel plate. There's a sliding seat to lie on. There's no danger at all."

"Bb-bb-bbut w-w-wh-what in th-th-th-the h-hhh-hhell do you steer w-with?"

"With your body. It's very simple. Now come on and unwrap your arms and legs from that post."

He pulled me out into the crisp Swiss morning air and took me down to the starting line, where I was introduced to a man named McCarthy, who is secretary of the Cresta Club and official timer and starter. He made me fill out a card for next of kin. The Cresta run was nothing but solid ice. I started to walk away but they caught me and carried me back.

"Wh-wh-wh-where's Gr-gr-gr-gr-gregory Peck?" I cried.

"He's coming," said Serge. "Now lie down on the sled. Hold on to the runners with both hands and keep your elbows in. Use the steel rakes on your feet to brake with. Look straight ahead and hold on tight. Go as fast as you want to. The ideal, of course, would be to crash the sound barrier, but if you don't do it on your first run, don't worry about it. Any questions?"

"Wh-wh-wh-where's Gr-gr-gregory P-p-peck?"

McCarthy rang the bell, Serge gave me a fast push and I was off. The skeleton started down at what is called Stream Corner at what I calculated to be three hundred miles an hour. I dug my rakes into the ice. Nothing happened. For two hundred yards straight down I hugged the sled thinking of absolutely nothing. I went under a road bridge and suddenly veered to the right on a sharp turn called Bullpetts. I straightened out, went under a railway bridge and then smashed hard against Scylla and was thrown over to a turn called Charybdis. Up until that time I was too frightened to think of anything, but just after Charybdis I had time to ask myself, 'Wh-wh-what in the h-h-h-hell are you d-d-d-doing here?"

After Charybdis the bottom dropped out and I whipped down Cresta Leap, which felt like a gentle 90-degree grade, on to the side of an ice mountain. As I gasped for air the skeleton returned to earth and the ride was over.

It took three men to pry my hands loose from the runners. I staggered back to the starting line. Serge was surprised to see me alive. But he wasn't discouraged.

"You did it in forty seconds. Now you have to do it *without* braking at all. Keep your feet off the ice."

Skeleton riding is a Swiss version of Russian roulette. I went down again, and then (a good psychiatrist could probably explain it), I went down a third time.

The next afternoon I was sitting in the lobby of the Palace again. Serge came in. But he ignored me this time and went over to a man who was just checking in at the hotel. All I could hear of the conversation was "Cresta Run," "safer than skiing" and "Gregory Peck is coming tomorrow morning."

SLOW TORTURE BY *TORTE*

THERE ARE many people in Vienna who consider the State Opera House the most important building in the city. But there are others of us, mostly on the highest cultural levels, who would trade three performances of *Fidelio* and two performances of *Lohengrin* for one plate of *Schlag* at Demel's, the grandmother of all Viennese pastry shops. Demel's is to Austria what the Tower of London is to England. Inside the hallowed mirrored walls are displayed the treasures of the country—foaming mountains of custard, strata upon strata of chocolate cakes, bottomless lakes of fruit-flavoured mousse, tunnel after tunnel of apple strudel and glaciers of ice cream and frozen tart.

It has been said that if Austria had an Aga Khan he

would be weighed each year at Demel's and given the equivalent in whipped cream and strawberry icing.

My initial visit to Demel's was an experience that could be put in the same class with the first time I met Ava Gardner or the second time I met Gina Lollobrigida. I went in with my eyes open, but it wasn't long before they became glazed and eventually shut.

The first thing I saw on entering Demel's was a large marble stand filled with homemade candies. On top of the stand was a handwritten sign advertising the speciality of the day. It was strawberry mousse with vanilla cream, grilled almonds and hazelnuts, sherbet and assorted candied fruits.

"A strong man," Si Bourgin, an International Food Patrolman, told us, "would quail at such a dish, but the average Austrian woman can eat three of them."

As my eyes became used to the light, I saw a room to the right with about twenty tables. The *décor* was late nineteenth century, and very little has been changed since Emperor Franz Josef used to pop in for an apple turnover. In the centre of the shop was the high altar. It was divided into two sections. One was devoted to sandwiches, cold cuts, salads, aspics and canapés. The other section was piled high with cakes filled with cream, cream filled with cakes, chocolate filled with nuts, nuts filled with chocolate, apples filled with pie crust and pie crust filled with apples. There were pineapple tarts, pecan nut rolls, lemon butter moulds, puff pastes, *Streusel* cakes, sweet crescents, plain *Gugelhupf* and complicated *Gugelhupf*, ladies' doughnuts, devil's doughnuts, *Anna Torten*, *Sacher Torten* and whipped cream in every shape and form.

I started to shake uncontrollably, and Bourgin had to slap me in the face to bring me back to my senses.

The women who wait on people are known as the Sisters of Demel's. They are dressed in shapeless black smocks and have all taken vows never to serve any pastry unless it has been made with butter. "Death before shortening" is their motto.

I chose five or six pastries as well as the *Anna Torte* (known as the most chocolate cake in the world), a large cup of coffee and whipped cream.

As I sat at a table and prepared to go to work, I heard a low rumbling, groaning and moaning.

"What's that?" I asked Mr. Bourgin.

"That's what is known as the Demel lament. Look around at all the women. You see them mumbling in German? Each afternoon they come here and as they eat they say, 'Oh, I can't eat this—it's so fattening. Oh, I can't take another bite, I shouldn't. Tomorrow I will eat nothing all day. I swear this is the last *Sacher Torte* I will touch for a month.' And so on. They never stop eating while they're talking. You could compare the Demel lament to a Gregorian chant. If an Austrian woman could not lament she would not come here."

"What kind of people do come here?"

"The Viennese aristocracy, tourists, beautiful women and people who are trying to forget their unhappy childhoods. You must never talk to a beautiful woman at Demel's. If she strikes your fancy you could send over a pound of butter with your compliments. If she accepts it you can then formally introduce yourself—but it must be done outside the shop. There is a back room known as the Rauch Salon, where you may take a pretty girl or an important business acquaintance. But it is very difficult to talk of love or business at Demel's."

I finished off the six pastries and *Anna Torte* and the coffee with *Schlag*. Before I knew it I was lamenting to myself. Bourgin carried me to the door.

I tried to apologize for my condition, but Bourgin would not hear of it.

"This always happens the first time someone visits Demel's. The *Schlag* just creeps up on you from behind."

Bourgin rolled me back to the Bristol Hotel. The *concierge* looked at me disapprovingly.

"Butterfat poisoning?" he asked Bourgin.

"Demel's," Bourgin replied.

The *concierge* nodded knowingly and rolled me up to my room.

Having survived the ritual trial by *Schlag* at Demel's, I felt ready to face the music. This was offered up on a silver platter with the reopening of the noble Vienna State Opera House. It was the greatest event in Europe since Queen Elizabeth's Coronation. Composers, musicians and many serious patrons of the arts like myself were on hand to participate in this glorious musical occasion.

The most beautiful women in the world, wearing more jewels per square seat than at any opera opening in the last fifty years, and the best-looking men, all in white ties and tails, applauded the opening-night performance of Beethoven's *Fidelio* lustily and with much gusto.

And speaking of white ties and tails, you're probably all wondering how I got mine. Vienna, whose name is synonymous with romance and easy living, does not make too many demands on its visitors. But at the reopening of the opera house, which cost $10,000,000 to rebuild and took nine years of sacrifice and hard work, it was thought that the wearing of a white tie and a tail coat was not asking too much. And it wasn't, if you had one. If you didn't, it was asking a lot.

By the time I arrived in Vienna, the diplomatic corps had raided all the rental agencies, and the closets were bare. You couldn't find a white tie or a black tail for love or money, or both. Vienna may have the greatest opera, but it has nothing to compare with Moss Bros., the impeccable London hiring service.

While pondering this situation a few mornings before the opening, I chanced to order breakfast at the Bristol

Hotel. When the waiter arrived, I was startled to see him wearing tails. I jumped up with elation and made the waiter stand at attention while we measured shoulders back-to-back. It was a perfect fit.

I started to negotiate over the rental, but the waiter informed me that his tails had already been promised to an Iron Curtain businessman who lived on the same floor. He did pass on the word, though, that the only tails left in the whole city belonged to a wine steward at Sacher's, and he thought I could get them if I ordered enough wine.

The wine steward, who hadn't been to Demel's for several months, was thinner than I was, but in Vienna there is a saying, "Opera lovers can't be choosers," and we made a deal.

The next problem was finding medals. You can't go in tails to the Vienna State Opera without medals on your coat. I was fortunate in finding the store that specialized in opera medals. I bought a good-conduct medal for having sat through an entire performance of *Parsifal* without coughing, a distinguished-service medal for seeing *Faust* fifty times, a Purple Heart for my foot's going to sleep during the second act of *The Girl of the Golden West*, and a Legion of Merit for holding the spear in Wagner's *Walküre*. I rented the white tie and vest and borrowed the starched shirt from a stuffed shirt at the American Embassy. Except for the wine card I carried in place of the opera programme, I could have easily been mistaken for Franz Josef's nephew.

So much has been written about the Vienna Opera, and so little about what it is like to go in a white tie and tails after a visit to Demel's! The first feeling I had was of listening to the Beethoven overture in an iron lung. When the curtain went up and I tried to turn my head, the shirt turned with it. As Fidelio entered upon the scene, my coat started to strain and groan. My shoulder blades started to cut a hole through the top of the jacket. When Pizarro made his entrance, a stud pin popped out, but my cuff links held fast.

In the second act, while Rocco and Fidelio were digging a grave for Florestan, one wing of my collar tried to take off, and during the "Leonora" overture, the vest buttons gave out.

The performance took twenty-one curtain calls, but I didn't have a chance to listen to the applause. I had to get the tails back to Sacher's. It was a memorable evening for those of us who could be there; Vienna lives again; Beethoven marches on; the opera touched the hearts of all of us; but the wine steward's tails at Sacher's will never be the same again.

THREE CLASSES FOR AMERICA

I WAS UNAWARE of it until recently, but a battle is raging throughout the Continent at the moment among members of the upper classes over who is in the upper class and who isn't.

From what I could gather it all started in 1954 when an English professor named Alan S. C. Ross wrote a paper that appeared in Finland titled "Linguistic Class-Indicators in Present-Day English." The professor made the point that the only way you can distinguish the upper classes is by their language (since they are not necessarily "better educated, cleaner or richer" than anybody else). He then went on to expound a very complicated theory showing that all you have to do is listen to a person and you know exactly where on the social ladder he belongs. Very few English aristocrats read Finnish papers, and if it hadn't been for that talented troublemaker Nancy

Mitford, the matter would have rested there. But Miss Mitford brought the paper back to England and threw it into the faces of the aristocrats. Then, to use a lower-class expression, all hell broke loose.

People who never listened to one another suddenly started to pay attention to what other people were saying. You can imagine what a frightening thing this was. The upper classes in England are now eliminating themselves by boring one another to death. Where it will end nobody knows. But other upper-class societies in Spain, France, Italy and Monaco are also worried about Professor Ross's paper. They reason that what's true for British aristocrats is also true for them, and while no lexicon on upper-class usage has been issued in any other language, it won't be long, the aristocrats think, until some smart aleck starts doing it.

An English aristocrat friend of ours was discussing the problem with us at Maxim's, where upper-class English usage is the common language.

"Of course you Americans" (British upper-class speakers always start a sentence with "of course you Americans") "don't have to worry about such things. You have no classes over there and nothing to distinguish yourselves by."

As much as we hated to admit it, the Englishman was right. America is a classless society. We have no one to look up to and no one to look down on. Financial wealth does not put you in the upper classes since there is no power with it. A rich man in America grovels at the feet of his servant. This could hardly be considered upper-class behaviour.

A person's pedigree plays no important part in American life. Americans don't care who their ancestors were. To us a Daughter of the American Revolution rates just as high as an usherette at the Brooklyn Paramount Theatre.

E

Most countries get their upper classes from upper-class universities. But America has no upper-class university. Some will argue that Harvard, Yale and Princeton are upper-class schools, but it's not so. Where do you find most graduates of these three universities? You find them riding the New York, New Haven & Hartford Railroad, hardly considered an upper-class line.

Perhaps America is lacking in class distinctions. We have no royal family except for Princess Grace.

At the risk of sounding like a radical, we would like to advocate that the United States adopt a class system.

The first question is who belongs in the upper class. Since there are so many opinions on this, the only fair way to decide is arbitrarily. All class systems are arbitrary, and there is no reason why America should be different.

The only solution is to do it alphabetically. Those whose last names begin with the letters A to H will be considered members of the upper classes, those whose names begin with I to Q will be considered members of the middle class and those whose last names begin with the letters from R to Z will be relegated to the lower classes.

Once the system is adopted no one will be able to change his name. The upper-class titles will go down through the male lines. Women, of course, can marry into another class.

Since there are class distinctions even in the upper classes, the people will rate starting with A. All one would have to do would be refer to his telephone book to find out where he stood in local peerage.

The upper classes will have priority for the best seats to shows, the best tables in restaurants and night clubs and in getting taxis. But they would also have responsibilities. Each year they must give a party on their estates for the lower classes, the R-to-Z people.

At first there may be some difficulties and friction among the classes, but eventually the I-to-Q people and the R-to-Z people will find their place, and we A-to-H people naturally hope they stay there.

No one can deny it will make American a much more interesting place to live in, and the Europeans can no longer accuse us of being a classless society.

It will bring all the Western countries closer together.

VIVE LE SPORT

THE SIX-MINUTE LOUVRE

Any sportsman will tell you that the only three things to see in the Louvre are the "Winged Victory of Samothrace," the "Venus de Milo" and the "Mona Lisa." The rest of the sculpture and paintings are just so much window dressing for the Big Three, and one hates to waste time in the Louvre when there is so much else to see in Paris.

Ever since the Louvre acquired these works of art, amateurs from all over the world have been trying to cut down the time it takes to see them. Before the war the world record was held by three Scandinavians, who had managed to make the course in seven minutes thirty-three seconds. This record stood until 1935, when a Britisher, Mergenthaller Waisleywillow, paced by his Welsh wife, did it in seven minutes flat. Waisleywillow in his first attempt made it in six minutes and forty-nine seconds, but was disqualified when he forgot to make a complete circle of the "Venus de Milo."

The record stood until 1938, when a Stockholm man, known as the Swedish Cannonball, introduced sneakers and make it in six minutes and twenty-five seconds.

That record stood during the war years, and it wasn't until 1947 that an attempt was made to beat the Cannonball. This time, because of the travel restrictions in Europe, the Americans had the course to themselves. The first one to take the Blue Riband to America was Tex Houston, from Oklahoma, who shaved two seconds off the record.

In 1949 a track star from Miami University (Ohio) made it in six minutes and fourteen seconds. In 1951, the Australians took the title away from the Americans with a six-minute-twelve-second Louvre.

By this time everyone was talking about a six-minute Louvre. Scientists said that under perfect conditions, with a smooth floor, excellent lighting and no wind, it could be done. But for four years no one was able to beat the Australians.

Then one Sunday I was tipped off that an American tourist was going to try for the record. His name was Peter Stone and he had made several previous attempts that had failed. Mr. Stone has been cited in many magazines and newspapers for a famous remark. After studying the "Winged Victory" for an hour, he said, "It will never fly."

He also was once asked to leave the Louvre when he said in a loud voice in front of a group of tourists who were looking at the "Mona Lisa": "I know the fellow who has the original."

Stone had brought his trainer along with him. He was wearing special indoor track shoes, and he had emptied his pockets of anything that would weigh him down. In choosing Sunday morning for the test he had banked on several things. One was that no tickets are required to get in and he would not lose precious seconds at the ticket booth.

Another was that the Louvre is pretty empty on Sunday mornings and most of the halls would be clear. In order to comply with all the rules, Stone had to get out of a taxi and tell the driver to wait. Then he had to rush into the museum, make the course, and get back in the taxi. The taxi had to be four feet away from the curb before he was officially clocked. Timekeepers from the American Express, Thomas Cook & Son and the French Bureau de Tourisme were on hand.

Stone received last-minute instructions from his trainer. "Whatever you do, keep away from the 'Rape of the Sabines' or you're a goner."

Stone wiped his track shoes in the box of resin that the Louvre keeps at the door for tourists and then got into the taxi. A gun went off and he jumped out of the taxi and rushed into the museum. The rule of the course is you must walk; you cannot run. Keeping his eyes straight ahead, he whizzed past the Salle Denon. At the foot of the Daru staircase, with just a glance at "Winged Victory," he turned left and rushed down two small flights of stairs past the rotunda straight to the "Venus de Milo." He circled the statue completely and headed back toward the "Winged Victory," shortcutting through the Roman and Greek antiquity rooms. His time was a fantastic one minute and fifty-eight seconds to the "Venus."

Stone took the stairs two at a time, stopped for two seconds in front of the "Winged Victory." He had a choice of two routes: the Salle Daru, where Napoleon I was being crowned, or the Salle Sept Mètres, where the Italian school was hung. He chose the Salle Daru, paused only for a second at the Napoleon painting and then rushed into the Grande Galerie, where "Mona Lisa" was waiting. In thirty seconds he was at the painting. The rules state that a contestant must make some innocuous tourist remark at the painting.

Stone said, "I don't see what's so great about it," and then wheeled, this time taking the Salle Sept Mètres. He rushed down the stairs, not even bothering this time to look at the "Winged Victory," hightailed it through the Salle Denon and was out in the street and in a taxi before you could say Leonardo da Vinci. As the taxi pulled away a gun was set off and Stone's time was recorded at five minutes fifty-six seconds, a new world tourist record. The Blue Riband was brought back to America.

Turning down offers from magazines and travel

agencies which wanted to use him for testimonial adver-
tisements, Stone modestly gave much of the credit to his
trainer.

"The next record I'm going after is St. Peter's in Rome,"
he said in an exclusive interview. "And then, who knows—
perhaps I'll try the Tower of London. They say you can't
do it in less than four minutes. Well, let's just see."

The champ threw his arms around his mother and the
photographers started taking pictures.

DELINQUENTS OF THE CHAMPS ELYSÉES

THOUGH PARIS has no Disneyland there are many
parks in the city where kids can get their kicks. One Sunday I took my two-year-old to the Champs Elysées park
on the Rond Point, just off the Avenue. The park, which
is a city block long, has a merry-go-round without music
where for twenty-five francs your child can ride a wooden
horse suffering from gout, or for fifteen francs he can push
a swing, or for thirty francs he can see a puppet show, or
for twenty francs he can sit on a park chair. There is a
sand pile in the centre of the park which is absolutely free.
The young coward I had in tow made straight for the sand
pile. It wasn't a question of saving his father money, but it
was the only place in the park where he could steal things
from the other children without getting caught. Paris has
no juvenile-delinquency problem, but most children under
five years old in the city are kleptomaniacs.

Joel had a pail and a shovel when he went into the fray,
but he set those aside immediately and grabbed a rake out
of the hands of a little French girl a half head smaller than
he. The little girl tried to take it back but Joel held fast.

I foolishly interceded and Joel broke into tears. He didn't expect to be betrayed from this quarter.

In between time a four-year-old who was sporting a bandaged ear took possession of Joel's pail and shovel. I interceded again on Joel's behalf. The four-year-old broke into tears and wouldn't give up the prize. I went to the mother to lodge a complaint but she said it was not her problem. She was seated with her husband, who was reading *Sport-Complet*, the French racing form.

He claimed it was not his problem either.

I was thinking of calling the American Embassy, but in the meantime Joel started throwing a doll at another French boy and had kicked in a sand model of Mont Blanc which three other French boys had taken all afternoon to build. With this evidence against me, I knew the American Embassy would be powerless to do anything.

Several French mothers were already talking in low tones about the *méchant garçon*. The two words you hear used in a Paris park over and over again are *mignon* and *méchant*. *Mignon* is used when referring to your own child; *méchant* when speaking about the other children in the park.

I took Joel's pail and shovel and showed him how to make a mud pie. I made one, then Joel made one, then I made one and then Joel took his pail and whacked a twelve-month-old blonde girl on the head.

An irate mother came off the bench, charging on to the field with a force of a substitute full-back, and accused me of trying to murder her child. I pointed out that it was very foolish of her child to stick her head in the way of Joel's pail.

Several other French mothers had joined the battle and while I tried to straighten out the matter diplomatically Joel took the little girl back to the sand pile and let her sit on him. This pleased the child immensely and everyone retired to their benches again to wait for the next outbreak.

I finally turned to the man who was reading *Sport-Complet* and asked him how a father should behave in the park.

"It is quite simple," he said. "I know French women. *Mon Dieu,* nobody knows them better than I. You make a mistake when you take your son's side in an argument in the park. You must always take the other child's side. Then the French mother will take your son's side. Instead of getting mad at your child, they will get mad at their own.

"Let me show you what I mean."

The man's son had just had his head caved in by another boy who had swung a wooden elephant at him. The man got up from the bench and went over and started scolding his own son. Immediately the mother of the boy came over and said the man's son was the innocent party and her own son was guilty. The man insisted his son was at fault, but the French mother said no it was her own son and, to prove the point, she started spanking the devil out of him. The man shrugged his shoulders, came back to the bench, winked at me, and went back to reading his *Sport-Complet.*

MAXIM'S AT FIFTY THOUSAND FEET

ONE OF THE ways that overseas airline companies induce people to fly the Atlantic is to appeal to their stomachs. The catering part of an airline has in recent years been given more and more attention, until today a passenger no longer asks how many motors a plane has, but what kind of soufflé it serves.

Pan American Airways, one of the major lines flying into Paris, has acquired the catering services of Maxim's, the famous restaurant on Rue Royale. It is not generally known how Pan-Am pulled this coup. As a matter of fact I believe this is the first time the story has been revealed.

When Pan-Am discovered, much to its surprise, that it would be permitted to fly into Paris, it tried to think of some novel way to attract business. The advertising agency, the publicity department, the sales force and Raymond Loewy were called in to think up an original plan.

But after two months of consultation, no one could come up with anything except the usual airline stunts of giving away free to each passenger a television set, or a new automobile, or a deep-freeze unit. None of these ideas was original enough and, with the deadline of the first flight only two months away, PAA officials were worried. Then one day when the gloom in the Forty-second Street offices was at its height, an elevator boy stuck a wrinkled slip of paper in the company suggestion box.

The next morning a hurried meeting of the board of directors was called and the suggestion was read: "Why knot getcha yorselves a famous Paris restorant too make the food? Signed Harry Otis, Elevator Boy No. 657."

At first there was silence, followed by the loudest applause ever heard on Forty-second Street. An idea had been born! So pleased was the board that it called in Otis, gave him twenty dollars and made him a vice-president on the spot.

The only Paris restaurant that anyone in New York knew was Maxim's, and without further discussion six executives, who hurriedly took a French course at Berlitz, were dispatched to Paris to make the deal.

But it wasn't as easy as Otis made it sound. When the executives arrived and went to Maxim's, they couldn't get past Albert, the famous but discriminating maître d'hôtel. After four days of standing on the Rue Royale they became discouraged and were going to find another restaurant.

Just as they were leaving, a man came up and asked them if they would care to buy any postcards of Paris

scenes. They said no, and the man asked if there was anything else he could do for them. One of the executives said
that they were unable to get into Maxim's.

The man looked up and down the street and whispered,
"Go in the side door through the kitchen." The executives
were so grateful that they gave the man seven thousand
francs and made him a vice-president on the spot.

When the officials discussed the plan with Monsieur and
Madame Vaudable, Maxim's owners, they at first met a
great deal of reluctance. Maxim's had served kings and
queens, princes and pretenders, brokers and buyers, but it
had yet to service aeroplanes. "How would a *filet de sole*
feel at twenty thousand feet?" "Was it possible for a
tournedos rossini to fly through fog?" "At what altitude
would a *homard à l'armoricaine* need oxygen?" "What
would be the reaction of a Beaujolais on taking off, and a
Pommery 1945 on landing?" "Would a truffle be ruffled in
a rain squall?" There were lots of questions that had to be
answered before Maxim's agreed to go along on the plan.

The officials, fighting against time, suggested that an
experimental flight be made with the food and wines, to
see the reaction in the air.

The day of the experiment was kept secret.

A special Stratocruiser was flown in from the States.
Police roped off Orly and all the planes of competing airlines were sent to Le Bourget. (It was reported another
airline had got wind of the stunt and had sprinkled dry
ice in the clouds over Orly, but it was never conclusively
proved.) An air lift of sixty planes brought in Pan-Am's
vice-president, and special bleachers were built in front of
the tower. The Army, which was also negotiating with
Maxim's to cook meals for the soldiers, sent a three-star
general, and the UN dispatched a commission to study the
experiment. No newspapermen, except this reporter, were
allowed near the field, and I received permission only after

I promised to hold up on the story until three months after the flight.

Since it was Otis's idea in the first place, it was agreed that he fly the plane. All unnecessary equipment was pulled out so there would be more room for food. The plane was loaded with *oeufs mayonnaise, thon, côtes de veau, entrecôtes,* steaks *au poivre, poulardes à l'estragon, terrines de canard, brochettes de rognons, champignons, choux de Bruxelles, fromages, patisseries* and every kind of French wine imaginable. There was only enough room in the plane for Otis and his radio equipment.

As Albert, who had also been made a vice-president by this time, shut the door, Otis waved once and took off into the sky-blue yonder. A loud speaker had been hooked up at the field and Otis's voice reported in every five minutes.

"This is Couvert Blanc calling Service Compris. I am at ten thousand feet; all is well."

The operations manager for Pan-Am was at a mike on the field. "Couvert Blanc, this is Service Compris. You are receiving fine."

Two seconds later. "This is Couvert Blanc. The *potage* has sprung a leak and is flooding the *coquille Saint-Jacques.* I am at eleven thousand feet."

One minute later. "This is Couvert Blanc. I am at fifteen thousand, the *bécasse flambée* is in flames, and the *canard à l'orange* has just lost its sauce."

The operations manager grabbed the mike. "Couvert Blanc, this is Service Compris. Don't, I repeat don't, take any chances. If the *foie gras* goes, come in for a landing. I repeat, if the *foie gras* goes, come in for a landing."

Five minutes later. "This is Couvert Blanc. I am at twenty-five thousand. A Châteauneuf-du-Pape 1924 has burst on me, the champagne is holding up well, the Burgundies are starting to rumble, and a Bordeaux is giving me trouble."

The operations manager looked worried. "Couvert

Blanc, please return to the field at once. Your life is worth more to us than all the *bouillabaisse* in Marseilles."

Ten minutes later. "This is Couvert Blanc. The *pommes soufflées* are deflated. The fire in the *bécasse flambée* has been extinguished. A case of Môet et Chandon has just fallen into the *foie de veau*. I'm going up."

One of the senior vice-presidents ran over to the mike and grabbed it away from the operations officer. "Otis, for God's sake don't do it. The experiment is a success. Land at once."

Otis just laughed. It was the laugh of a man who didn't know what the word danger meant. "I'm going up to fifty thousand. No one knows what a *bœuf Stroganoff* will do at fifty thousand and this is as good a time as any to find out."

There was complete silence for three minutes. The spectators held their breaths and then, as clear as a bell, Otis's voice came over the loudspeaker.

"It's okay. The *bœuf Stroganoff* is okay. I'm coming down."

There was a loud cheer that could be heard all over Paris. When Otis, who had gained a little weight on the flight, got out of the plane he was given the Legion of Honour, and besides the rank of vice-president, which he already held, he was made head *sommelier* at Maxim's. It was the least they could do.

GLUG! GLUG! GLUG!

I RECENTLY HAD my first taste of water skiing on the Riviera. (It tastes like salt water.) Water skiing is fast becoming one of the most popular sports along the Mediterranean. Statistics show that this year on the Côte d'Azur there are more cowards water skiing than there are doing the breast stroke.

Monsieur Pierre L'Eau-Froide gets credit for originating the sport about twenty-five years ago, though there are some who claim he invented it by accident. The story goes that M. L'Eau-Froide, who was snow skiing in the Alpes-Maritimes, came barrelling down a mountain so fast that he couldn't stop himself and went right into the Mediterranean. At this very moment a speed-boat was going by and threw him a rope. Instead of sinking, M. L'Eau-Froid stayed up on his skis and went flying through the water.

"What are you doing?" Elsa Maxwell, who was on a cruise, shouted to him.

"I'm water skiing," he shouted back.

Thus water skiing came into being.

M. L'Eau-Froide would have gone on to be the greatest water skier in the world, but unfortunately when the speedboat slowed down his boots were too heavy and he started sinking into the sea.

"What are you doing now?" Miss Maxwell shouted.

"I'm skin diving," M. L'Eau-Froide gasped as he sank for the last time.

M. L'Eau-Froide would have probably been given credit for inventing skin diving also, but for the fact that his detractors pointed out that when he sank he still had all his ski clothes on, so obviously there was no skin diving involved. But let the future sportswriters fight that one out.

As I said before, I went water skiing for the first time and I recommend it to anyone who loves the taste of the open sea. My mentor was Roy Evans, who owns the Racquet Club in Miami Beach. Mr. Evans is a big promoter of water skiing. It was from his club that Miss Dolores Kipple water skied from Miami to Nassau across the choppy Gulf Stream on one ski in ten hours and twenty-five minutes.

Mr. Evans was looking for someone to do the same thing from Cannes to the Suez Canal, providing, of course, the Egyptians would give me a visa. We went out in a motorboat. Mr. Evans gave me my instructions: "Just put on the skis in the water and sit on them. When I throw you the rope, hold on to it, but push with your legs and remain seated until I signal you to stand up. Don't stand up right away. Are there any questions?"

"Can I wear a life preserver?"

"No, it will slow you down. Remember, push with your knees and sit down on the skis."

Mr. Evans threw me into the water, and the water skis after me.

It's about as easy to put on skis in the water as it is to eat a snail with a salad fork.

I finally managed to do it by hanging from the motorboat upside down while Mr. Evans slipped the skis on.

Once my feet were in the skis it was a simple matter to push me off into the deep water.

I was just getting settled on the skis when Mr. Evans threw me the rope. He put the motorboat into high gear and away we roared.

You learn many things when you are water skiing. The first thing you learn is not to keep your mouth open when you start off. It is amazing how much salt water the human body can swallow when it wants to.

"SIT DOWN! SIT DOWN!" Mr. Evans shouted.

I didn't hear the rest of what he was saying. You never do when you're twenty feet under water.

The next time I tried it I was doing well until one ski headed for the Suez Canal while the other turned toward Gibraltar. It probably would not have been serious except my feet were in both of them.

On the third try I managed to get up on both skis and for the first time realized what a thrill water skiing was. There you are, skidding along the water at twenty-five knots, your head in the wind, your legs beating against the waves. Once you get the knack of it, it's as easy as—glug, glug, glug, glug, glug, glugglugglug glug.

THE PINCHING PARROTS OF ROME

IF YOU ASK an American to name the most sinful city in Europe, the chances are he'll say "Paris." He might be right, but when it comes to *public* naughtiness, I believe that Rome has it over any other city on the Continent. Perhaps it's that the Romans have been at it longer.

Whatever the reason, reports have filtered back to the United States that girls in Rome were being stopped on the streets, pinched on buses and streetcars and arrested for kissing in public. Since so many young American daughters had been planning to visit the Eternal City, it was only natural that American parents should be concerned. I was therefore asked to go to Rome and investigate. I was told money was no object to long as I got the facts.

I spent two weeks researching. I talked to girls who had been pinched, to the boys who had pinched the girls, and to the policemen who had pinched the boys. I rode hundreds of miles on streetcars and buses, motor-scooters and bicycles, observing and doing, and although my wife hasn't talked to me since, I feel I now know the *real* Rome —the Rome that is not in the guide-books.

The most popular outdoor sport in Rome is *pappagallismo*. The men who participate are called *I Pappagalli della Strada*, or The Parrots of the Street. The parrots of Rome differ from the wolves of most other countries in that they talk to pretty girls instead of whistling at them. The Italian man, when he sees a beautiful woman, cannot refrain from complimenting her. He will tell her she is as beautiful as a movie theatre, or as lovely as an Alfa Romeo automobile; he will compliment her on having had parents with the good sense to see that she was born, and he will regret that he is not a cobblestone so the girl could walk on him.

The lawyer, the doctor, the aristocrat, the workingman, the schoolboy . . . all qualify as *pappagalli*.

The technique, like the cast of characters, varies widely. One type of parrot will walk at a woman's side, sometimes for miles, whispering beautiful words into her ear, often praising her attributes in great detail. Another type may prefer to tramp along behind the woman, reciting his litanies and phrases of adoration aloud. Women are also followed by men driving cars or motor-scooters, the modern Italian version of the Roman chariot. Such men are prevented by circumstances from whispering; they must shout their praise, in order to be heard over the roar of the engine.

Miss Gianna Segale, a very pretty young Italian actress, says: "Recently a man got out of his car and started to follow me. He told me he was in love with me, and by the time we had walked seven blocks he proposed marriage. He followed me all the way home and when he saw my mother he asked her for my hand in marriage. The next day I received a beautiful bouquet of flowers. That night he came to the house, but I wasn't home. My mother let him in—and he proposed marriage to *her*."

Another Italian girl told me she was shopping one morning around nine-thirty and a very nice Italian man complimented her and invited her to have a cup of coffee. She accepted because he looked pleasant and respectable. He said he was a law clerk and she asked him, "But don't you have to get to work?"

He replied, "If I said I was sick they would probably fire me, but if I say I stopped to have coffee with a beautiful girl, they will understand."

Generally a parrot will give up the pursuit when a woman pays no attention. If the man gets too fresh, she can usually get rid of him by turning on him and shouting; he'll flee before the police arrive (in Italy, as in most other countries, the woman in such an incident always gets the benefit of any doubt). But most of the women I spoke to in Rome said they're pleased, rather than annoyed, by the *pappagalli*.

Lois Maxwell, the American movie actress, who has been living in Rome since 1949, said, "It's great for a woman's ego when she is complimented by a stranger; but Rome spoils a woman for the northern countries. England is terribly dull; a man might walk two blocks before he turns around and looks at you."

Some parrots like to yell at girls who are driving cars. Miss Maxwell reports that when she stops her car for a red light she hears many flattering remarks. One day I rode with her and a kerbstone admirer shouted, "Oh, if I could only be your chauffeur, I would drive you—I would drive you mad!"

Pappagallismo in Italy is not a fad but a tradition. No one knows when it started, but Dante wrote in 1300:

> So gentle and so honest appears
> My woman when someone salutes her
> That her mouth's trembling becomes dumb
> And the eyes do not dare to look.

The eyes of modern Italian women apparently are more daring. They look. A young doctor I know gave me some instruction in *pappagallismo*, and followed with a demonstration.

"You must use imagination," he said. "Watch me. You see the pretty girl coming down the street. First I pass her without saying anything. Now, quick, we must cross the street and walk fast."

The doctor rushed across the street, walked swiftly, and then recrossed and started up the other side so he would meet the girl again. As she approached he stopped in surprise and said, "But hello! It's so nice to see you again."

The girl looked puzzled. She had seen him before and was trying to remember where. The doctor finally admitted he had mistaken her for someone else, but he was not sorry, because this other girl could not compare in beauty with the present young lady, and even if he had made a mistake it was fortunate one. He asked her to have coffee with him. She refused with a warm smile; she had to go home, she said.

The doctor was not discouraged. He told me, "The next time I see her she will have coffee with me. She knows I am not a bad sort. Most Italian men are too impatient. If you are patient all good things will come to you."

Sue Graham, an American working in Rome, said the *pappagalli* do not distinguish between Italian girls and foreigners.

"The trouble is that if you are accosted by one Italian man and you ask the help of other Italian men in shaking him, you then have trouble getting rid of your rescuers."

Pappagallismo is not a serious police problem; a policeman will interfere only if a woman complains to him. If an Italian man wishes to flatter a woman on the streets, it is felt that there is no reason for the law to butt in. It makes the man feel better, it makes the woman feel better, and it certainly makes life more interesting.

Next to pappagallismo, the most popular sport in Italy is the *mano morta* or dead hand—the gentle Italian art of pinching. Most *mano morta* takes place on the streetcars and buses, particularly during the crowded rush hours. The method was explained to me by Jean Giovoni, an airline public-relations girl.

"You are riding a crowded bus and you have to stand. Suddenly there's something—a hand or a brief case? So you hold on to the strap with one hand and try to push aside the brief case with the other. But it is not a brief case. So you look around and try to discover who it is. The faces are noncommittal, and you don't have many choices of action. You can slap the face of the man nearest you, but he may be the wrong one. You can make a scene, but it is doubtful that the other passengers will do any more than laugh. Or you can get off the bus, which can get very expensive after a while. So you just shrug your shoulders and stay where you are."

My bachelor doctor friend also considers himself an expert on *mano morta*. "You must look very nonchalant," he said, "even bored, if possible. You wait until the trolley goes over a bump or stops abruptly. Then you pinch— gently. If the woman protests, you can reply, 'I was not pinching you, I was trying to steal your pocketbook.' This will make the other passengers laugh and they will be on your side."

Are American girls in danger of being pinched?

"No," said the doctor. "American girls rarely ride the buses or streetcars and besides the majority of them are too thin."

The police report that one of the favourite ruses of Roman pickpockets is to use a pretty girl on a bus as a decoy. While a man is pinching the girl the pickpocket is pinching the Romeo's pockets. Men who complain to the police that they have been robbed in such a manner rarely get much sympathy.

In discussing the pinching procedure with one of the Via Veneto café parrots, I was told, "It's silly to write about pinching in Rome. You'll give people the wrong idea. We Romans don't go around pinching girls. Maybe perhaps we pinch a little in the spring, but that is only because we're happy with the sun and the warm weather. Women have been covered with heavy clothes all winter and suddenly you see them in summer dresses, beautiful and fresh, and then perhaps you just want to give them a little pinch. But it is not because we are bad. We feel good and this is the only way we can show it."

Pinching, like *pappagallismo*, has been going on for a long time in Rome and probably will continue to thrive as long as there is standing room on the buses and streetcars.

Of course, there are certain legal restrictions. They were explained to me by Carlo Rimini, one of Rome's leading lawyers.

"The law of Public Security of June 18, 1931," he told me, "says that it is forbidden to molest a person in a public place or in a place open to the public. For example, if a woman is followed insistently by a man who speaks to her, in spite of the fact that she has repeatedly expressed her will not to be molested, that man can be considered a troublesome, importunate person and a violator of the law.

"If a man addresses himself to a woman who passes by, using an expression which—even if containing appreciation for her beauty—rouses her resentment, the man can be prosecuted at the woman's insistence."

And, Mr. Rimini said, it is a crime to force a woman to be kissed in public. "Naturally, it is a crime to insult a woman in public—and a simple kiss given in public, when this has been given suddenly and against any expectation of the woman, is considered by some courts as an insult."

But the law that irritates both the young men and young women of Rome is a law against kissing even if both parties are in consent. This law has been on the books since 1931, and although the Fascist régime was tough about it, enforcement was relaxed just after the war and up until 1949.

Then the Christian Democrat party started to enforce it again and thousands of young lovers have been fined for kissing.

A special squad of police called the Good Custom Squad is charged with preventing outward displays of emotion in the city's parks and along the streets and highways. If a man and woman are caught kissing, they are given a ticket and fined three hundred lire (forty-eight cents) on the spot. Originally the fine was fifteen hundred lire each and the tickets were sent to the lovers' parents. But there were so many protests and the courts were so jammed that the new method and lower fine were substituted.

Many young people are still bitter about the law, though. "What do they want us to do?" one youthful bachelor asked. "We aren't murdering anybody. Bad woman can walk around Rome without being molested, but a good girl who is caught kissing her boy friend in the park is embarrassed and humiliated."

Of course the law has not stopped necking in Rome; it has just made the youngsters more careful about picking a place. One of the favourite spots is the historic Appian Way. Every night the sides of the road are crowded for miles with automobiles. The police try to patrol the Way, but with little success. As soon as one car spots the cops, the driver starts honking his horn in warning. Other cars pass the signal along, and the whole Appian Way becomes a bedlam. But no one gets fined.

My young doctor friend said he knew all about the law and had even been fined twice himself. "But I finally found the solution," he said proudly. "The only place where you can safely kiss a woman in public in Rome is the railroad station. The cops assume you are saying good-bye to someone and even the Italian police would not prevent you from kissing a dearly loved one good-bye. So I take all my girls to the railroad station. I find a nice warm bench and nobody bothers me. We could sit there all night and no one would say anything. But if we walk out of the railroad station and I so much as have my arm around the girl's shoulder, immediately we get a fine."

Americans are not safe from the law either. A young American girl I know was walking one night near the Colosseum with her American boy friend and just before they reached the Temple of the Vestal Virgins they kissed each other. An arm came out of nowhere with a policeman at the other end, and tapped the boy on the shoulder. The cop said in Italian that kissing was forbidden and asked them both to come down to the police station. The girl started to cry and the boy protested in English that in America kissing was legal, in France kissing was legal, even in Russia (he wasn't sure here, but he took a chance) kissing was legal. Why, the boy demanded, was kissing not legal in Italy? The policeman was young and the argument was strong so he finally let them go with some vague advice about "*sempre coperta*" ("always under-cover") and walked away down the path.

Is it safe for an American girl to come to Rome? Of course it is. And exciting, too. Roman men mean no harm, and there are few places in the world where a woman will get as much attention as she will in the Eternal City.

But a word of warning. Do not be guilty of the error a young lady from Smith College committed last spring. She accepted the kind offer of a young Italian man to show her through one of the art galleries. The Italian spoke no English and the girl no Italian, so as they went from paint-ing to painting the Smith girl kept saying in her best French, "*Très bon, très bon, c'est magnifique.*"

After a while, however, the man asked her a question very remote from the subject of art. The girl, thinking he was still talking about the paintings, again said in French, "Very good, very good. Magnificent."

A policeman not far away heard her scream and came running. But when they got down to the police station and the man explained his side of the story, the police chief laughed and dismissed the case.

"In Rome, my child," the police chief said, "you must be very careful when you say, '*Très bon.*' . . ."

A FLEA IN THE OINTMENT

At the Cirque d'Hiver in Paris they made a film called *Trapeze*. As it was being directed by Sir Carol Reed and was starring Burt Lancaster, Tony Curtis and Gina Lollobrigida I thought I'd stroll over and help myself to an eyeful. I discovered almost everyone scratching himself or herself. On making discreet inquiries I was told that it was fleas.

"Speak to Mr. Mankowitz," someone told me. "He knows more about the fleas than anybody."

I found Mr. Wolf Mankowitz holding a straw which had a flea perched on the edge. "Up, boy," said Mr. Mankowitz. "Up on your silly hind legs, or I'll swat you."

Mr. Mankowitz gave the flea a rest while I talked to him.

"Yes, it's quite true. The place is lousy with fleas. The animals brought most of them and then we've had actors and actresses in this picture from all over the world. I was originally hired on this picture to write dialogue, but when the flea thing happened they put me on that problem. I still don't know how we're going to lick it. As a matter of fact, it has got completely out of hand."

"When did you first discover the circus had fleas?"

"Well, Sir Carol Reed and I came early to look over the circus and left with an entire family under each arm. Sir Carol took them back to the George V with him, where his wife, Lady Penelope, was staying. It was she who made the discovery. We thought the fleas were mosquitoes. Lady Penelope thought differently. I'm afraid the poor girl was right."

"How many fleas would you say are here at this moment?"

"Counting the extras?"

"Counting everything."

"About 6,800,756. Of course, that's just a rough estimate."

"It must be very difficult for the people to work."

"Well, that isn't the problem. It's the international ramifications we're worried about. If the story ever gets out to the papers we're sunk."

"For example?"

"Well, take Sir Carol, for instance. I think he'd better tell you himself."

Sir Carol came over, scratching.

"Tell me about the international flea ramifications," I said.

"Well, I can only tell you my wife's part of it. She left the other day for London to visit her mother. A few days later her mother went to visit the Governor General of Malta, who is her brother. There was no stopping her. I'm afraid the Cirque d'Hiver fleas have started their own circus in Malta."

"That's only part of it," Mr. Mankowitz said. "Kirk Douglas came on the set the other day wearing a beard for his part in a film on Van Gogh. He left with about seven fleas in his beard. Now it looks as if our fleas are going to be in his picture."

"And then a model from one of the big fashion magazines took some fleas back to the *couturiers*. As far as we know some escaped into the clothes and we don't know where those fleas will eventually wind up."

"Does Burt Lancaster have fleas?" I asked.

"Only when he's up on the trapeze. He seems to attract the high-flying type of flea. On the ground they stay away."

"What about Miss Lollobrigida?"

"Why don't you ask her?"

I went over and asked Miss Lollobrigida if she had fleas.

"Not so far," she said.

"Have you ever had fleas?"

"Yes, I think so."

"When?"

"It's hard for me to remember."

Mr. Mankowitz pulled me aside. "Do you know why all those fellows are standing around Miss Lollobrigida?"

"Why?"

"Because there is a rumour that if a virgin flea bites Miss Lollobrigida, and then bites another person, that person will inherit the Colosseum in Rome."

"Is that the truth?"

"Yes, but it has to be a virgin flea. There was one flea that bit Miss Lollobrigida and then went out of his head and started to bite other fleas. We had to kill him."

"Will the fleas keep increasing as the picture goes along?"

"I'm afraid so. When you have two torsos like those of Lancaster and Curtis and a figure like Miss Lollobrigida's around there is nothing for the fleas to do but increase. The thing to worry about is not what will happen during the picture. With Sir Carol's mother-in-law spreading them in Malta and Kirk Douglas spreading them at Arles and the rest of us going back to England, Hollywood and Italy, it won't be long before the whole world is flea-ridden.

"The only thing to do," said Mr. Mankowitz, "is to start the picture from scratch, and we've done that already."

THE DUNKING OF
KATHARINE HEPBURN

Miss Katharine Hepburn was in Venice making a film version of the Broadway play *Time of the Cuckoo*, which was renamed *Summer Madness* for the movie audiences. I was fortunate to be on location with her when she had to fall into a Venice canal for a scene in the picture. Now there aren't many people who have seen Miss Hepburn fall into a canal and I must admit it gave me quite a thrill.

Before the scene I had a chance to discuss it with her and she told me this was the second time she had to go in. David Lean, the director, said he wanted to shoot the scene from another angle and Miss Hepburn said she didn't mind.

"Isn't the canal dirty?" I asked.

"We don't think about that," she said. "Last week when I fell in I came out with half a water melon in my shoe. But I've met dead rats and dead cats in Long Island Sound, too, so who am I to complain?"

"It smells a little like Long Island Sound at that," I said.

"It doesn't smell as bad as that cigar you're smoking. That's the foulest-smelling cigar I've ever seen in my life."

I threw the half-smoked cigar into the canal.

"Miss Hepburn," I said, "since this movie is about a secretary who comes to Venice to find romance, why don't we cook up a story about you giving advice to American secretaries who come to Venice to find love."

"Oh, for God's sake!" she said. "Somebody take this man away. Can't you do any better than that?"

I needed my cigar bad.

Miss Hepburn told me she had fallen in love with Venice and the people. "They're the most artistic race in the world," she said. "They all paint and they're so charming and generous and their romantic enthusiasm is something unbelievable."

The actress had already learned to speak Italian.

"I had to learn it in self-defence. For the first few days the Italians kept saying to me that I must be *stanco*. I didn't know if they thought I was drunk or just playing the scenes badly. Then I discovered *stanco* meant tired."

"How does Venice compare to Africa?" I asked her.

"I was crazy about Africa. I love to travel anywhere someone else is paying the bill. Venice intrigues me. I can't get over the fact that men would dare build a city from a swampland. How they did it is something I'll never know. I just love to float around the canal at night."

"But do you enjoy it alone?"

"Anyone with any brains learns to enjoy things alone. Besides, you can pick up anyone you want in Venice. The second night I was here I met an Italian boy who showed me the entire city."

"Isn't that dangerous?"

"No. I pick up people everywhere. I haven't the time and I can't be bothered to be suspicious of people."

The scene was about to be shot and Miss Hepburn went to put on her make-up.

David Lean, the director, told me, "She is one of the finest and easiest artists I have ever worked with. She has tremendous talent. This is a damn hellish picture to do because we're shooting most of it outside, but she never complains and she never shows temperament."

Miss Hepburn came back wearing a beautiful white organdie dress. The scene called for her to be taking movies of a Venice street while backing into a canal. That's when she falls in.

Before going on the set she took one look into the canal and said, "My, it's filthy."

I followed her gaze. Among the things I saw floating on the surface were: some orange peel, two plums, a pigeon feather, a wrapper from an ice-cream popsicle and my half-smoked cigar.

Miss Hepburn went on the set, rehearsed for scene one, and then as the camera turned she went back, back, back, right smack into the canal. She swam ashore while the spectators applauded.

They wrapped a towel around her and led her away to a hot bath. The only thing that puzzled me was how a woman who would fall into a canal like that could object to one little Italian cigar.

ONLY ONE OF EVERYTHING

CARY GRANT, when he was making *The Pride and the Passion* in Spain, estimated he had been interviewed 1,346 times since he arrived in Europe. Having also made *To Catch a Thief* on the Riviera, he felt he had a great deal of experience in dealing with the European press, and as a public service to the Screen Actors' Guild in Hollywood, Mr. Grant is distributing, at his own expense, a form interview which can save time and money for every actor and actress coming over here to make a movie.

This is the type of interview Mr. Grant warns the Hollywood star to expect:

"Señor Grant, is this your first visit to Spain?"

"*Si.*" (When answering yes or no, always speak in the language of the country.)

"What are your impressions of Spain?"

"I cannot say enough about Spain."

"But how does Spain compare with other countries you have visited?"

"Why should one want to compare Spain with any other country?"

"What do you think of Frank Sinatra?"

"There is only one Frank Sinatra."

"What do you think of Sophia Loren?"

"There is only one Sophia Loren."

"What do you think of Stanley Kramer?"

"There is only one Stanley Kramer."

"What was the best film you made?"

(At that point, Mr. Grant recommends that the star plug the picture he has a piece of. If there are several, he should plug them all.)

"What do you think of European women?"

"America will never be able to pay the debt it owes to European women."

"What do you think of Marilyn Monroe?"

"There is only one Marilyn Monroe."

"What do you look for first in a woman?"

"Intelligence, beauty, charm, kindness, and usually I look to see if the seams of her stockings are straight."

"What does a woman look for in a man?"

"His tie. When a woman is in love with a man, she is afraid to show it, so she looks at his tie. When she isn't in love with him she doesn't care to look at him, so she looks at his tie."

"What is your favourite dish?"

"*Paella.*"

(Unless you have stock in some food company, Mr. Grant recommends you mention the national dish of the country.)

"If you weren't Cary Grant, who would you like to be?"

"A brave Spanish bullfighter."

"What country has the worst movie industry?"

"I would not like to answer that question."

"What are your favourite books?"

"The Spanish classics."

"What is your favourite music?"

"Spanish music has always been my favourite. I am a great admirer of Manuel de Falla."

"Do you have a bad temper?"

"Only when I see a bad bullfight."

"What makes you happiest?"

"To see a good bullfight."

"What is the most moving thing you remember?"

"The first time I saw Spain from the air."

"What is your favourite animal?"

"The Spanish burro. I have always admired the strength, the tenacity and the kindness of the Spanish burro. To me, he represents all the finest qualities of a beast of burden."

"What do you think of the Spanish press?"

"There is only one Spanish press."

I FOUGHT WITH ALEXANDER

SOME TIME AGO a United Artists drumbeater called me up and said, "As you know, Robert Rossen is making *Alexander the Great* and we are arranging a junket of hand-picked journalists to tour Greece with Arnold Toynbee, who will point out all the great battlefields. Are you interested?"

"Has Toynbee said he'll go?" I asked.

"No, but the hand-picked journalists said they would."

Three months later the same man called me and said that Toynbee had "chickened out" (a military expression meaning he wasn't going) and the Greek trip was off. The film was being made in Spain anyway, because Spain looked more like Greece than Greece did. A few weeks afterwards the man called again.

"Rossen is marrying off five thousand virgins in *Alexander the Great* in one of the greatest scenes ever filmed in movie history. A hand-picked group of journalists has been invited to attend the wedding."

"Who's he marrying them off to?"

"Five thousand Greek soldiers. You see, according to history, Alexander wanted to mate the East with the West, and he decided to make his soldiers marry Persian women —the offspring would be the twain that were never supposed to meet."

I calculated that even if the press agent was exaggerating by double, that still left a marriage of 2,500 virgins to 2,500 Greek soldiers—a figure which could not very well be ignored.

But when I arrived in Madrid I discovered that I had been taken in. Rossen was making a film called *Alexander the Great* but he wasn't marrying off any virgins to Greek soldiers.

"I do have a mass wedding in my picture, but it won't take place for a couple of weeks and as far as I know Alexander never specified what kind of girls he wanted for the wedding, as long as they were Persian.

"This week we are filming battle scenes. As you know, Alexander fought the Persians and Greek mercenaries at Granicus and routed them in his famous human-tank attack. As long as you're here, why don't you fill in as a Greek mercenary?"

"How much does it pay?"

"A dead Greek gets $4.80 a day, a dead Greek lying in the water gets $5.50; a Persian soldier on horseback gets $6.00, a dead Persian gets as much as a dead Greek; one of Alexander's men who doesn't speak gets $3.95; a refugee from a battle gets $3.80. We are using eight hundred soldiers from the Spanish Army and they are getting $1.50 a day. Take your choice."

I told Rossen I'd rather be a live Greek than a dead Persian floating in the water and he agreed to pay me $3.95. Since I was a hand-picked journalist it was decided to put me next to Alexander in the battle line-up. Alexander was being played by Richard Burton, the Welsh actor who began his epic career in *The Robe*. The battle was to be fought on a plain just outside of Madrid, near the airport.

On the big day I was delivered to a tent at eight o'clock in the morning for make-up and costume. I was thrown a helmet, a spear, a sword, a grey tunic and a shield. Franco's army and cavalry arrived and they were divided up, half to play Persians, half to play Greeks.

Mr. Rossen was riding around on a palomino pony getting his shots lined up. Mr. Burton was playing cricket behind his tent; the British camera crew was drinking tea. The air was filled with the tenseness that usually precedes a great battle.

I practised throwing a spear at a dead tree trunk (the dead tree trunk was getting $2.50 a day), and I took several swipes with my sword at a chair reserved for Claire Bloom, who was playing the female lead.

At eleven-thirty we started to line up for the battle—Persians and Greek mercenaries on one side of the river, Alexander and good Greeks on the other side. The sound of American, English, Italian and Spanish voices rent the air. The horses whinnied and the sheep bleated, three planes took off from the airport in succession. Mr. Rossen drew up his palomino pony in front of the CinemaScope camera, dismounted and prepared for action. I aimed my spear at a Greek mercenary and waited for Mr. Rossen to give the word.

Mr. Burton moved in beside me.

"Be careful of these Spaniards," he whispered. "They think they are really fighting a battle and you're liable to get hurt."

"Fear not, Alexander," I told him. "We'll be eating Darius's cavalry for breakfast and we'll be spitting Greek mercenaries out of our teeth in the morning."

"I'm not talking about the Greeks and Persians. I'm talking about the Spaniards. Those extras are crazy. They start swinging swords and spears and no one knows who's going to get hit. In our last battle they carried five men out and the doctors had to put twelve stitches in one of them."

Rossen was shouting for us to keep quiet. "Have we got enough blood on the set?" he asked the make-up department.

They said there was enough blood.

"Okay, give Alexander a large wound in the leg."

I lifted my spear to protect him, but somehow the make-up man fought his way through and splashed blood all over Burton's thigh.

"Somebody tie a bandage around Alexander's leg," Rossen said. "You there" (he pointed to me), "tie a bandage around his leg."

"Which leg?"

"The one with the wound on it."

"Do as he says," said Burton. "Then maybe we'll be out of the fight. I'll ask for you to stay behind with me to tend the wound."

"What about the Persians?"

"They're not Persians, I tell you, they're Spanish extras and they're going to make a *paella* out of us."

"Okay, anything you say."

Rossen rehearsed a scene with Alexander and General Memnon, the Athenian who was in the pay of the Persian Emperor Darius. In it Memnon, played by Peter Cushing, comes to Alexander and asks for quarter. Alexander refuses to give him quarter and Memnon goes off to fight and die. While Alexander talked to Memnon I was supposed to wipe the blood off Burton's leg.

Just before the scene started I whispered to Burton, "Why don't you give him quarter? Then maybe the battle will be called off."

He whispered back, "Rossen doesn't want me to give the Persians and Greek mercenaries any quarter."

"That's fine for him. He doesn't have to face those Spanish extras."

The scene was played beautifully and Memnon rode back across the river to make his last stand. Suddenly Rossen gave the signal for Alexander's men to attack the Persians. About six hundred grim-faced extras on each side started to square off, throwing spears, swinging swords and dropping rocks.

"Come with me!" Burton shouted, and we both jumped down behind a large rock and hid from the director.

"Victor Mature taught me how to do this," Burton said to me. "When the scene is over we'll put dirt on each other and Rossen won't even know the difference."

We threw dirt and some more blood on each other, and by the time Rossen yelled "Cut!" we looked in pretty bad shape. The battlefield was littered with Spanish extras holding their heads in their hands and moaning and groaning. The Persian cavalry had gone off into the hills, completely routed.

We walked back to where Rossen was standing.

"Nice work, boys," he said.

Burton winked at me. I helped put a Spanish extra on a stretcher and then got in line with some "dead" Greeks and Persians who were waiting to get paid. It was hard to take, but almost every one of them got more money than I did.

BULLS

THE TALK around the bullfighting circles of Madrid is that the bulls aren't as brave as they used to be. The explanation may lie in the fact that most bulls receive no instructions before entering the bull ring. Millions of words have been written on how to be a brave matador, a brave picador and a brave sicador (one who gets sick at a bullfight), but not one word of advice has ever been written on how to be a brave bull. Perhaps this sad state of affairs can be remedied. The following advice is for fighting bulls only.

The first thing you've got to realize is that you're a bull —you're a wild, noble, honest animal who has been bred, not for his meat, but for his courage. You are endowed with keen instincts, physical soundness, pugnacious arrogance, ferocious bravery, bull-like nobility, and when it comes to plain good looks you've got it over any other four-legged male in the world.

You've come from a long line of fighting bulls and you should be as proud of them as they hope to be of you.

For the last five years you've done nothing but eat and sleep and it's been a good life. But now the time has come to bid farewell to the ranch and the many dear friends you must leave behind. A brave bull, when leaving the breeding ranch, walks straight up the wooden ramp to the truck, never looking behind. If he falters or hesitates, his owner may think him a coward, and there is nothing more horrible for a bull than for an owner to think he's afraid.

You arrive at the bull ring tired and in need of a shower. The handlers unbox you and put you in your own corral, where you can wash and be refreshed. Because you're going to fight the next day they don't let you out in the evening.

The next morning you're up bright and early and you're excited. This is it; this is what you've been waiting five years for. Today you're going to have a chance to appear in front of twenty-five thousand people who have paid up to ten dollars a seat to see you fight. You say to yourself, "If only Dad could have lived to see me now."

You eat a light breakfast and then the fight promoters come into the corral and start pairing you off with another bull. Each matador must fight two bulls, and since there are three matadors on the programme, that means five other bulls as well as yourself are chosen. There are a couple of spare ones in case one of you loses your nerve, but it rarely happens.

You don't know how it happens but the day just flies by. Before you know it, it's five thirty. You can see through the slats in your box that the stadium is full. A band is playing and most of the people are in their shirt sleeves. They're in a gay mood, drinking wine and eating peanuts and shouting to each other. You start perspiring a little, not from fear, but from nervousness. Your blood tingles and your heart starts beating fast. You keep saying to yourself, "Is this really happening to little old me?"

Suddenly you hear trumpets and drums. The horse gate next to you opens and the matadors, banderilleros, picadors and ring servants parade into the ring to the president's box. You have a new respect for tradition.

Then you see two teams of three mules each, richly tasselled and belled, and you wonder what part they play in the bullfight. You find out sooner than you think.

The moment is near. The matadors bow to the crowd. They exchange their dress capes for fighting capes, and strut up and down in front of the beautiful women and retired bullfighters. It makes you mad to see this display of conceit and you can't wait to get your horns into the seat of their pompous pants.

A bugle sounds, the gate swings open and at last you

rush into the ring. The crowd roars a cheer, the like of which you've never heard before. They're cheering you. You're so happy you want to sit down and cry. But a brave bull has to stay on his feet and you run around snorting and raging and drinking in the glory. As you run around you see a pink cape out of the corner of your eye. It's as though someone were waving a red flag in front of you and suddenly you're furious. You dig in your front hoofs and charge for the cape.

The thing that you, as a brave bull, must always keep in mind when a fight is on is that it took generations of careful breeding and scientific know-how to make you what you are today. For the next twenty minutes you have a chance to repay your owner for all the care, affection, kindness and money he has lavished on you for the past five years. No other animal except a fighting bull is given such an opportunity.

As we mentioned before, the first thing you must do when you charge out into the arena is snort and kick up your heels and charge into the fence a couple of times so the matador who is hiding behind a wooden fence can study you for any defects. He wants to know on which side you hook, how wide your horns are and if you have a tendency to chop. Don't tell him anything. And don't waste your energy on the peon. The crowd doesn't care if he gets gored or not

Now the matador will come out. He does some experimental cape work with you and you might as well go along with it. If you don't, the audience may ask the president to send in another bull. (Besides, it gives you a good chance to study the weaknesses of the matador.) After making a few passes and getting the feel of the cape, the signal is given to let the picadors into the ring.

The real show is about to begin.

The picador, with his wide-brimmed hat, canvas pants and armoured legs, is the meanest man in the bull ring, disliked as much by the audience as he is by the bulls. He is mounted on an old blindfold horse, and since the animal is not long for this world, there is no harm in goring the poor thing and putting him out of his misery.

Once you get the horse it's only a matter of seconds before you get the picador, and the crowd will be with you all the way. A brave bull should never hesitate when charging the picador. He should charge right in, aiming for the underside of the horse. At first the pick will sting a little, but you'll be so furious by this time you won't even feel it.

Some picadors (what are we talking about, most picadors) will try to work their picks into your flesh, and this makes the crowd very mad. When you hear a roar from the fans you know the picador is not playing the game and anything you do to him will be all right with them.

The idea behind "picking" you is to weaken your neck mucles so you'll keep your head down. There's nothing wrong with this except for the way the picador does it.

After he's finished, the banderilleros come out and stick barbed sticks in you. They are supposed to correct your faults (as if you had any). After the picador you hardly feel the barbs and, since it adds colour to the bullfight, there is no reason for you to object to them.

The final act is about to take place. This is the act that separates the bulls from the calves. This your chance to show how brave you really are. From now on it's you or the matador, and almost everyone is rooting for you.

In this stage you are more dangerous and wary than you have been before. You're on the defensive, and we hate to mention this, but you're also fighting for your life.

The matador carries a scarlet cloth called a *muleta*.

The cloth is folded and attached to a stick, which the bullfighter can use with one hand. The matador, bareheaded, walks over to the president's box and asks if he can kill you. This makes you laugh. He then dedicates

you to someone in the ring, usually a beautiful lady.
If you wish, you can dedicate the matador to somebody,
but you usually don't have the time.

Now the matador approaches you (don't go to him; it
makes him look good and you can save energy this way).
You face each other. The first pass you'll probably make
is the *pase natural*. It's very dangerous and beautiful when
done right. Try to get as close to the bullfighter as possible
without touching him. If you do it right the crowd will go
mad. Now turn around and do it again. "*Olé!*" they're
shouting. Do it again and again. Now take a short trot
around the arena and take a bow.

The matador will adjust his *muleta* and you get back to
business. He may try a chest pass, at which time you pass
the matador's chest and keep going straight out. You'll
probably be doing many variations of the different passes,
but in order to look good you must stay as close to the
bullfighter as possible. When you get bored with running
back and forth you might try to gore him. The best place
to gore a matador is in the chest. If you don't want him
to die you might try for the groin. Toss him up in the air
and then stomp on him. The crowd will go wild and
you'll be the hero of the day.

If you don't gore the bullfighter, then you must face
what is known in bullfighting circles as "the moment of
truth." At this moment the matador stands in front of
you, his sword raised, staring straight at you while you
have your head down (that damn' picador). The matador
suddenly runs at you and, thrusting the sword with valour
and skill, he pushes it between your shoulder blades, cutting the big blood vessels of your mediastinum.

If he makes a good thrust you should drop dead on the
spot.

Sometimes the matador misses and then the spectacle
becomes cruel. You start coughing up blood and all the
fight has been taken out of you. The crowd is very mad

when this happens and they hate the matador almost as much as you do.

If you don't die right away they give you the *coup de grâce*, but you have to lie down to get it. You might as well, because if you don't, the matador will be sticking swords in you all day.

Once you're dead, those beautiful mules run out into the ring and your feet are hooked to the chains. If you've been a brave bull then you can savour your greatest hour of glory. The mules will drag you around the ring while the crowd screams its approval. It's a very moving scene.

If the matador has done well, they'll cut off your ears and give them to him. It really doesn't matter. At this stage of the game you can't hear anything anyway.

THE MAKING OF *MOBY DICK*

WE WERE invited to attend the launching of John Huston's film *Moby Dick*, which was being shot, in part, in the sleepy town of Youghal (pronounced you all), Ireland. Mr. Huston had transformed Youghal into New Bedford, Massachusetts, because he claimed that Youghal looks more like New Bedford in the early nineteenth century than New Bedford does.

The transformation was not only a physical one but a sociological one as well. Before Mr. Huston selected Youghal, this town, with a population of five thousand, 144 miles from Dublin, had been fighting a losing battle against unemployment, poverty and emigration. About seventy years ago it was an important Irish seaport, but as silt and mud filled up the harbour, Youghal lost its shipping industry and, in a way, its spirit.

The townspeople, who had never seen a movie camera

before, much less a live Hollywood actor, suddenly found Youghal the most talked-about place on the Irish map.

Pat Dooley, the local contractor, was given the task of making the Youghal Quay look like New Bedford. Paddy Linehan's combined pub, butcher shop and slaughter-house became headquarters for the actors and crew.

The British Legion Hall was repainted and turned into offices for the production. Large barrels of Guinness were rolled on to the dock to represent whale-oil barrels. Sailing ships were brought in and anchored in the harbour. New England had never seen anything like this.

Mrs. Rohan, who runs the stationery shop, sold out every autograph book she had, and had to send to Dublin for more. She also sold one hundred copies of *Moby Dick*. As the town took on a New England atmosphere, tourists from all over Ireland poured in to see the making of the "fillum," as it is called in Youghal.

Paddy Linehan, who formerly sold six barrels of stout a week, began averaging thirty-two barrels. The turf accountant (Irish bookie) said his business had doubled. A police force was sent in from Cork because Youghal police couldn't handle the traffic or the crowds.

You would be thinking that everyone in Youghal would have been happy over the arrival of *Moby Dick*, but such was not the case. Take Bill Kavanagh, for example. Bill Kavanagh owns a pub about two hundred yards from Paddy Linehan's. When Pat Dooley, the contractor, came to see Kavanagh about painting his pub for the fillum, Kavanagh said his pub didn't need any painting and if they were going to paint it they could just as well pay him seventy-five pounds or forget about the whole thing. Now as everyone in Youghal knows, there has al-ways been bad blood between Pat Dooley and Bill Kavanagh and so it came as no surprise that Pat Dooley said he didn't need Bill Kavanagh's pub in his fillum, and he was not about to sign any sort of guarantee with Kavanagh in case the pub was damaged.

So what did the fillum company do? They blocked off Kavanagh's pub from the quay and then it was Paddy Linehan who was getting all the business and Bill Kavanagh who was cursing the day *Moby Dick* ever came to Youghal.

I went into Kavanagh's pub to talk to a few of Kavanagh's loyal customers. Sure and they gave me an earful about the fillum.

How many people showed up at the town hall for jobs as extras when the call went out? Two thousand, that's how many. But did the fillum people take the poor people? They certainly did not. They took the bank clerks' wives, and the participants' wives, and left the poor people's wives and kids out in the cold. That's what they did, said the people in Kavanagh's pub.

And when it came to carpentering and painting, did Pat Dooley hire the people who were unemployed? He did not. He hired the factory workers from the textile plant who were on vacation. That's what Pat Dooley did.

Bill Kavanagh did the right thing when he refused to let the fillum company use his pub, said the customers. When it's all over his roof will still be in good shape, and he won't have no cheap paint on his building. Paddy Linehan may have the business now, but the customers will be coming back to Kavanagh's as soon as all the nonsense is over. That's what they said in Kavanagh's pub.

But it wasn't Bill Kavanagh who was the saddest man in Youghal. The saddest man was Kevin McCarthy. When it was first announced that *Moby Dick* would be fillumed in Youghal, McCarthy discovered there was a part in the picture for a man with a wooden leg. Since McCarthy was the only man in Youghal who had a wooden leg, it was obvious he would get the part. And while thousands of citizens were queued up in front of the town hall begging for parts, Kevin McCarthy walked about safe in the knowledge that his part was guaranteed.

The only man he feared was Patrick Kennedy, his life-long enemy. If Patrick Kennedy found out about the need for a man with a wooden leg, McCarthy was sure Kennedy would cut off a good leg just to spite him.

But McCarthy, alas, did not get the part, and it wasn't because of Kennedy either.

The part went to Gregory Peck, who played Captain Ahab, the one-legged tyrant of the *Pequod's* crew and the leading character in Mr. Huston's fillum.

Moby Dick turned half the adults and all the children of Youghal into autograph hounds. A stranger walking through the streets suddenly would find himself surrounded by people shoving books and papers at him and begging him to sign them. The more he insisted he had nothing to do with the picture the more they pleaded for his signature.

It was under these circumstances that I found myself signing books by the hundreds. At first I signed my own name, but then, when I saw the disappointment on the faces of the children, I took the liberty of signing more valuable names. I alternated the signatures between Tony Curtis, Glenn Ford, Humphrey Bogart and Jerry Lewis. The pleasure the youngsters got from reading these names in their books more than made up for any discomfort I suffered or buttons I lost in the process.

One group of bobby soxers surrounded me just as I was going into Linehan's pub.

"Would you be knowing Gregory Peck?" a pretty colleen asked.

"That I do."

"And would you be telling us what he's like?"

"I will. Gregory Peck is an honest but not a very talkative man. He's modest and true and a friend, and thinks kindly of all people. I'm proud to be knowing him."

"Oh, it's just what we thought," said another little girl. Then, sighing, she added: "If Gregory Peck was only Catholic."

It would only be natural that a few of the people in Youghal would be letting the filming of the picture go to their heads. I was having a pint in Linehan's and listening to an elderly citizen talk about the bygone days of the town.

"Ah, yes, lads, it seems like only yesterday, though it must have been fifty years ago, that Captain Moby Dick sailed into this very harbour and unloaded his cargo of whale oil right out there on the quay."

As a matter of fact, there are not too many people in the town that know Moby Dick was a whale and not a person. Kevin McGlory, an assistant director with the company, took advantage of the situation and began signing all autographs "Captain Moby Dick."

There are about forty-four pubs in Youghal plus many other drinking places, and not all of them were doing as well as Paddy Linehan's. As a matter of fact, the west end of town was extremely quiet, and the pub owners there lost all their customers to Linehan's.

How did they feel about it? Mr. Dempsey, at Dempsey's pub, said, "I'm not complaining. We get the circus down here and the fair, so if Paddy Linehan gets the movie it all evens itself out at the end of the year. It's bringing money to the town, isn't it?"

Paddy Maher was not as broadminded about the whole thing.

"I'll not be commenting about the competition. I'm a little disappointed in the boys, but the fillum can't last forever and the west end of town will be flourishing again.

If there's been any unfairness it can be laid on the heads of the Cork County Liquor Commission, which allows the pubs around the fillum to open at seven a.m. in the morning and not have to shut down until midnight.

"But worst of all they've given the pubs a dispensation on Sunday to be staying open. Now where does that leave the rest of us?"

A townsman said that he thought that many of the busloads of people who had come from other parts of Ireland were just as thrilled with the pubs staying open on Sunday as they were with the making of the film.

Even the priests of the town were happy about *Moby Dick*. I spoke to one of them who was taking a photograph of Richard Basehart. He said, "The farmers have been complaining because there's nobody to bring the wheat in, and that's a bad thing. But if God saw fit to bring John Huston and Gregory Peck to Youghal, and put our poor town on the map, then we can only offer our thanks. I wonder if you'd be asking Mr. Basehart if he'd give me his autograph?"

MY FAVOURITE TOURISTS

ONE OF THE traits I like best in American tourists is their use of protective camouflage to blend into the local setting. A good example of this fine art was recently provided in Paris by Mr. Oscar Serlin, the Broadway producer, and his wife. One night they went to the Belle Aurore for dinner. Seated at the next table were four Americans, two women and two men, who apparently had just arrived on the boat.

One of the party said, "Aren't you lucky? We're the only Americans in the place."

A woman in the group, looking over at Mr. and Mrs. Serlin, said, "Look at that cute French couple. Get a load of her clothes. You don't see clothes like that back home."

"And look," said the other woman of the quartet, "how seriously the man is studying the menu. Let's order exactly the same things he orders."

Mr. and Mrs. Serlin were very nervous by now, but Mrs. Serlin whispered to her husband not to let on that they were Americans. Mrs. Serlin, whose French is nearly perfect, ordered the hors d'œuvre, *poulet Armagnac*, asparagus and the *patisserie maison*.

One of the American men called over the waiter and said, "We want the same thing they're having."

The four Americans smiled at Mr. and Mrs. Serlin, and the producer and his wife smiled back.

"They probably saved up a month's salary to come here," one of the Americans said.

"I don't know," one of the women replied. "She's got very nice jewellery on. You know, some of the French do have money. He looks like a doctor or a lawyer."

"He's probably a farmer. They are the ones who have money in France. Look! He's studying the wine list now. Isn't it exciting?"

Mr. Serlin, who was now starting to enjoy himself, ordered the most expensive wine on the card.

"The *même chose* for us," one of the men shouted to the *sommelier*.

The four smiled at Mr. and Mrs. Serlin, and the producer and his wife smiled back.

The hors d'œuvre arrived and everyone started to eat.

"Isn't it interesting," the man said, "that in France the women order the food and the men order the wines?"

"Do you think the woman with him is really his wife?" one of the women said.

"Oh, for heaven's sake," the other replied. "I'm sure it is."

"I wouldn't be too sure. You know how these Frenchmen are. But she's wearing a wedding ring."

"That doesn't mean anything in France. Did you read *Bonjour Tristesse*?"

The wine arrived and everyone's glass was filled. One of the Americans raised his glass in a toast, and, smiling at Mr. and Mrs. Serlin, said, "*Vive la France.*"

Mrs. Serlin, rising to the occasion, raised her glass and said, "*Vive l'Amérique.*"

"Aren't they darling?" one of the women said.

"Look how he's testing the wine," the man said. "He can really tell if it's good or not."

"I'll say this for the French. They know how to eat."

Mr. Serlin started testing his *poulet*, and his wife whispered to him, "Stop hamming it up."

While they were eating the asparagus, one of the Americans raised his glass and, smiling again, said to the producer, "*Bonne santé.*"

Mr. Serlin replied, "I dreenk to zor good halth."

They all laughed and drank again. "I'll bet that's the only English he knows," the lady said.

The dessert arrived and everyone seemed satisfied.

"*Vive le* Mendès-France," one of the men said to Mr. Serlin.

"Mendès-France isn't the Premier any more," the other man said.

"Who is?"

"I don't know. I think it's Pinay."

"*Vive le* Pinay."

Mr. Serlin raised his glass. "*Vive le* President Truman."

Just as Mr. and Mrs. Serlin were leaving, one of the men called over the maître d'hôtel and said, "EXPLAIN TO THEM WE WANT TO BUY THEM A DRINK."

Mr. and Mrs. Serlin smiled and the four smiled back.

"*Vive l'amour*," the man said.

"*Vive la compagnie*," Mr. Serlin said.

They drank up, shook hands all around, and the producer and his wife left. As they walked out of the door,
one of the men said something to the other three and
winked.

Everyone at the table laughed.

Another one of my favourite American tourists is Mr.
Emil Oppenheimer, a retired sausage manufacturer from
Oak Lawn, Illinois. Mr. Oppenheimer, who used to make
over 100,000 pounds of sausage a week, now spends his
time travelling, making friends for America by the car-
load, and enjoying all the wonderful sights that Europe
has to offer.

The last time I saw Mr. Oppenheimer—in the lobby of
the Excelsior Hotel in Rome—he was wearing a green
chequered peaked cap with a red pompon on top, a pink
sports shirt and a dark chequered sports jacket. This time
he was wearing a green chequered peaked cap with red
pompon on the top, a pink sports shirt and a dark
chequered sports jacket.

"I like to travel comfortably," the heavy-set traveller
told me.

"How was your trip over this year?" I asked him.

"Just great, son, just great. I took the S.S. *Constitution*
this time and met a titled Englishman. When we shook
hands I thought I had hold of a jellyfish. I also met an
inspector from Scotland Yard, and a movie star. Nothing
much happened. But after we were at sea for a few days
I met a 100 per cent hotsy totsy Yankee Doodle Dandy
Boy who came up to me and said, 'I hear you're a world
traveller' (meaning me). 'I just bought a new Chevvy so
I need someone to travel through Spain with me. Let's
get off at Gibraltar and drive together.' The ball and
chain was against it, but I said okay. What a mistake.

"First thing the British asked us for an exit visa at
Gibraltar and the guy has none. He has no permit for his

radio and no driver's licence. I try to help him out, but he says to me, 'Who needs you?'

"At the Spanish border our troubles really started. The guy has Florida plates and his papers call for Pennsylvania plates. He has a Chevvy and his papers call for a Plymouth. I finally passed out some pesetas and we got through.

"But then at Malaga we got lost and went to a police station. The captain of the police assigned some booze-house bum as an interpreter. Well, the dive he took us to was something to write home about. The pay-off came when the guy who owns the Chevvy hires the bum to take him to Cannes. We left him there and went on our own.

"The trains in Spain are nothing to write home about—lousy is the word—except maybe for a couple of Diesels. We went to Cordova. Don't recommend Cordova to anyone. It's nothing. Then we went to Madrid and saw bull-fights. For a sausage manufacturer it's not very interesting. I've seen better performances at the Chicago stockyards. From there we went to Tangier. Saw nothing but phony shows put on for tourists. Don't go. It's not worth it. Criminal is the word."

"Where did you go from there?" I asked, to show I was still listening.

"Florence, and then to the opera at La Scala in Milan. It was better than the bullfights, but you have to like opera. I don't like opera. Then we went to Salzburg and Berlin. You got to be careful in Berlin or you'll wind up in Commie territory. The Mrs. is always looking for weird *objets d'art* so we picked up some crazy guy as a guide and he said he knew where they were. The Mrs. wandered into a Russian building by mistake and the nut started screaming his head off. So did the Russians. The guy pulled her out and bawled her out in German. She don't know German or Russian, and so she started crying. That guy sure was a nut. We found nothing, so he took us to a

famous coffee house where the greats hung out in the past.
It might have been great in the past, but it was nothing
to see now. The guy ordered a couple of sandwiches for
himself and some chocolate bars which he stuffed in his
pocket. He said he wanted them for his mother.

"We got back to the hotel and the Mrs. says, 'Let's get
the hell out of here.' I agreed. Berlin you can have.

"Then we went to Stuttgart. It was nothing. Then to
Baden-Baden."

"Nothing?" I asked.

"You're right. And then to Paris. We saw *La Bohème* at
the opera last night—an amateur performance."

"Well, Mr. Oppenheimer, it looks like you've been
really enjoying yourself in Europe this year."

"Couldn't be having a better time. We're going to England and then back home. I don't expect much from
London. That's another nothing place."

"Do you plan to come over again next year?"

"Sure," he said. "Why not?"

ADVENTURE IN HYDE PARK

On one of my periodic expeditions to London I ran
smack into a Bank Holiday week-end. A Bank Holiday
week-end is a raving tourist nightmare. It means that all
banks are closed, which means that all legitimate busi-
nesses are closed, which means that there is absolutely
nothing to do from Friday until Monday except sit in a
London park and stare at birds.

Bird watching comes easy to my family. My grandfather
was one of the most promising bird watchers in London,
until the day my grandmother caught him in Hyde Park
staring through his binoculars at the third floor of the

Grosvenor House Hotel when he was supposed to be watching the hovering tactics of two young chiffchaffs of the three-leaf warbler family. But that's another story.

Since my bird watching has grown somewhat rusty of late, I purchased two very interesting books on the subject. One was Bruce Campbell's *Bird Watching for Beginners* and the other was R. S. R. Fitter's *Pocket Guide to British Birds*.

Mr. Campbell sets the tone of the sport in his first sentence when he warns that "even though more people are interested in wild birds than ever before, it still takes courage to be a bird-watcher." Mr. Fitter is much more encouraging and assured the reader that if he studies his lessons and keeps his notes in order, it will only be a short time before he will recognize the difference between the hovering of a kestrel and the plummet diving of a gannet. This I found hard to believe.

The basic needs of a bird watcher are a pair of binoculars and a pad and pencil. I borrowed the glasses from Mr. Frederick Tupper, a famous horse watcher who wasn't going to the track that day, and stole the pad and pencil from the Savoy Hotel.

Hyde Park was crowded when I arrived and almost every bench was taken. Since bird watchers usually have better luck behind rocks, I chose to hide behind a small grey stone, my eyes trained on a small bush, my ears strained for the love call of a hawfinch, or the agonized cry of a lesser redpoll.

Four hours later, my knees a little weak and my eyes a little inflamed, I saw my first bird.

At first I thought it was a bearded tit, but Fitter proved me wrong. The bearded tit has a call note of a rather metallic "ching, ching, ching" and occasionally emits a "dru-dru" sound. This bird made a "chack-chack" sound and issued other harsh and unprintable noises. I checked Fitter and found a picture of a bird that bore a very close resemblance. It was a red-backed shrike and looked almost like a cock kestrel because of its chestnut back. But the thing that gave him away was that he was much smaller and had a small hooked beak.

I made some notes:

Observation No. 1: Time 2.05; male bird landed on bush, went "chack-chack."

Observation No. 2: Time 2.06; he has rufous brown and creamy white feathers with a blue head and a black stripe through each eye. His slightly hooked beak is black. Fitter says its a red-backed shrike. I must go along with him.

Observation No. 3: Time 2.09; bird, disturbed by children's screams, hopped to another branch. He's looking straight at me. I stare back.

Observation No. 4: Time 2.15; I finally stared him down. He had to look away. I laughed out loud. He flew away.

An hour later I saw a common redstart. His chief notes were 'hwee-tucc-tucc" and he sounded common. As everyone knows, common redstarts are famous for their squeaky warbles, and this bird was no exception. I thought he'd drive me crazy with his singing. The common redstart has a curious habit of shivering his tail and loves to catch flies (who doesn't?). He strutted up and down the bush, showing off with his singing, and finally flew away when I threw a rock at him.

I thought I caught a glimpse of a rosy starling, but Fitter says it's doubtful. They're rare birds and often confused with ordinary starlings, which can be seen anywhere.

In the next hours I saw twelve London pigeons, two common sparrows, and, though Fitter might doubt me, I'm sure I saw two little bustards. At least they looked like bustards to me.

It started to get dark and I was just about to call it quits when all the lights in the Grosvenor House Hotel went on. Only then did I realize why my grandfather liked to do his bird watching in Hyde Park. I also realized why Campbell said it took so much courage to be a bird watcher. You can't imagine how many bobbies patrol Hyde Park at night.

THERE GOES MY BENTLEY!

ANYONE WHO thinks that life in the International Set is all fun and games is suffering from a delusion. I can assure them that it's strenuous work. An average season includes Drag luncheons, Drag dinners, polo matches, horse shows, the Grand Prix, a party at Elsa's, a party at Aly's, a cocktail at Rosita's, a ball for the Duke and Duchess, supper at Arturo's, lunch at Pam's and a hay ride with the Derby winner.

Aly Khan's annual party at the Pré Catelan, given after the Grand Prix, traditionally ends the fiscal year for the International Set. Old romances are terminated, new romances are started, and it gives the women members an opportunity to wear the jewels they have received during the previous year.

Immediately after the party, the annual business meeting is held, and since I have been serving as acting Secretary of the International Set I shall rattle off the minutes of a typical year's meeting.

"The gathering opened with a vote of thanks to Cartier's, Christian Dior, Balenciaga, Van Cleef & Arpels, and the Rolls-Royce Company for making deliveries on Saturday.

"A motion was introduced to censure authoress Nancy Mitford for writing in the *Sunday Times* that Marie Antoinette, 'putting class before country, sent military secrets to the enemy through her lover, Fersen, and deserved a traitor's death.'

"One of the hottest debates of the year ensued. Miss Mitford was accused of cutting the ground from under the European aristocracy.

"A French countess said it was a 'cruel and beastly thing to write.'

"The only one who came to Miss Mitford's defence was an English duchess who said, 'We've always been critical of Nancy because she's more French than English. But this time we're pleased with her. I, for one, have always thought Marie Antoinette was a stinker.'

"When it was discovered that Miss Mitford was in Greece it was decided to table the motion until her return, at which time she could either defend her position or be cashiered.

"Several members complained they were being seated next to tourists at Maxim's, and it was agreed to send a stern note to Albert, the maître d'hôtel, advising him of the situation.

"The question of home-breaking and husband-stealing was brought up by several of the wives. They stated that there were some women in the International Set who weren't playing the game. The wives asked for stricter enforcement of the rules concerning the theft of husbands.

"The home-breakers (there were more than I imagined) stated through a spokesman that all was fair in love and war, and if the wives could not hold on to their husbands, then they didn't deserve them. The husbands seconded the motion and the wives were defeated by two to one.

"A motion was then made by the husbands to introduce younger females into the International Set. It was defeated by both the wives and home-breakers two to one.

"Complaints were voiced by several members that wealthy Greek shipowners were building such elaborate yachts that it was very hard for the ordinary millionaires to keep up with them. One Greek shipowner, complained an oil tycoon, even had an aeroplane on his yacht. The Greek shipowner defended himself by saying, 'Sometimes I like to sail and sometimes I like to fly. I never know until I get up in the morning.'

"A compromise motion was introduced and passed limiting each yacht to one aeroplane.

"The Greeks walked out of the meeting.

"The Secretary proposed that all yacht owners should adopt a united stand in limiting their crews to five Jaguars on any cruise, so as to give guests a better chance of getting their Bentleys on board. The motion was carried by acclamation.

"A French marquise brought up the question of buying titles. 'All the South Americans are buying titles and I think a stop should be put to it,' she said.

"It was pointed out by one of the members that the South Americans were contributing large sums of money through parties and gifts to the other members of the International Set. The French marquise said if they wanted the titles so badly they could marry into them, as the Europeans did.

"The South Americans walked out.

"At the end of the meeting the president of the International Set described the programme for the coming year. It was as exciting as any programme could be, with 896 cocktail parties, 564 dinner parties, 453 buffets, 230 charity balls, Drag luncheons, Drag dinners, polo matches, a party at Elsa's, a party at Aly's, a cocktail at Rosita's, a ball for the Duke and Duchess, supper at Arturo's, lunch at Pam's and another hay ride with the Derby winner."

Whenever my yacht needs a new paint job and whenever I run low on caviar and peacocks' eggs, I tie up at Cannes for a few days and make a tour of the Riviera.

The biggest difficulty, of course, is to get my Bentley off the boat without scratching it. If the crew were only half as careful unloading my Bentley as they are with their Jaguars I would be very happy. But these are difficult times and a coward must put up with many inconveniences unheard of before the war.

The Riviera has changed so much since the days when an Englishman spent twenty-five guineas for breakfast instead of twenty-five guineas for a two-week holiday. Now almost everyone, except the British, has money to spend and one has to wait in line with the *concierges* and chauffeurs to play the roulette at the Palm Beach Casino.

Of course there are still some good people left. In Cannes I saw Elsa Maxwell, the Duke and Duchess of Windsor, James Donahue, Mrs. Donahue, Aly Khan, Baron de Rothschild, Jack Warner, the Eric Loders and several other friends I know and love. But I must face facts. My Riviera isn't my Riviera any more. The beaches are filled with beautiful women from the provinces, many without any pedigree at all. The bar at the Carlton has signs all over it that the customers must drink up a minimum of 150 francs, and the movie crowd has taken over almost every table.

I found Eden Roc much more to my liking. There I saw my own kind. There were Elsa Maxwell, the Duke and Duchess of Windsor, James Donahue, Mrs. Donahue, Aly Khan, Baron de Rothschild, Jack Warner, the Eric Loders and many other people I know and love.

Eden Roc is the perfect luncheon spot. There is a bright blue swimming pool, a charming restaurant, a cool, clear bay and a Van Cleef & Arpels jewellery shop within two minutes' walking distance of the pool.

No minimum at the bar here. No maximum either.

If anyone wants to see young people having fun, I suggest he have his chauffeur drive him to Juan-les-Pins. It isn't wise to wear too many jewels when going there. A sporty diamond pin or emerald bracelet will do the trick. The most popular clubs in Juan-les-Pins are Maxim's, the Vieux Colombier and the Hollywood Casino. These clubs seem to be popular with all classes of society and prices compare favourably with Monseigneur's, Florence, and Jimmy's Club in Paris.

Maxim's has an audience-participation programme and in spite of everything I found myself laughing at the proceedings. It was jolly good fun. Sidney Bechet and Claude Luter were the featured instrumentalists at the Vieux Colombier, which gets a very interesting clientele.

After all the light fun, one can retire to the Juan-les-Pins Casino. On ordinary evenings the play is rather primitive, but there are gala nights when many interesting people show up, such as Elsa Maxwell, the Duke and Duchess of Windsor, James Donahue, Mrs. Donahue, Aly Khan, Baron de Rothschild, Jack Warner, the Eric Loders and several other friends I know and love.

When I tired of dining at private villas, I drove over to Beaulieu for dinner at La Réserve and also to look in on the Casino. Charming place, Beaulieu, and people shouldn't miss it.

Of course, the real treat of a trip on the Riviera is the Sporting Club at Monte Carlo. It is situated right on the water and one knows exactly who's in town by identifying the yachts in the harbour. One still dresses at the Sporting Club, which keeps out many of the people you wouldn't want to have at the Sporting Club. But at the same time it is a wonderful place for friends to meet such people as Elsa Maxwell, the Duke and Duchess of Windsor, James Donahue, Mrs. Donahue, Aly Khan, Baron de Rothschild, Jack Warner and the Eric Loders.

I'm back on my yacht and I've had a lovely time. Many of the best people are leaving for Biarritz and Deauville now and I don't want to be left here alone. So I'll just say

good-bye to Cannes for the moment as soon as the crew
gets my Bentley and their Jaguars aboard.

"Be careful, boys, you'll scratch it."

LOUIS XIV IN VENICE

PROBABLY THE worst thing that ever happened to my
pride as a respected member of Europe's International
Set was when Don Carlos de Bestegui gave a costume
party in Venice and forgot to invite me. The party was the
talk of two continents and I think I was the only member
of the International Set who hadn't been asked. At first,
I thought it was some careless secretary's mistake; so as
soon as I arrived in Venice I took out my Louis XIV
costume and went over to the Labia Palace to correct the
oversight. But Don Carlos himself told me that it was not
an oversight and that he had never had any intention of
sending me an invitation to his housewarming. I told him
that the 30,000,000 readers of my paper wanted to hear
about the party and he said to me: "There will be princes
and princesses, dukes and duchesses, marquises and
millionaires, and they're not interested in what the press
has to say."

The next day I saw de Bestegui and asked him again.
"Why is everyone interested in my party?" he said. "It's
just a small, modest affair. A little housewarming. I can't
see why they should get so excited everywhere. If you want
to come, you'll have to arrive before eight-thirty and I'll
put you in a room upstairs until three o'clock. Then
maybe I will let you come down and talk to a few guests,
but be sure and eat your dinner first."

The next day Don Carlos denied that he had promised
me admittance and said that if I came he wouldn't let me
in. The following day he said that it was all right for me to

come at ten o'clock and twenty minutes later he denied saying that. The only decent thing left to do was crash the ball.

At seven-thirty sharp, dressed in the full costume and wig of Louis XIV, I climbed into a motorboat and set sail from the Lido for the Bestegui Labia Palace. I won't deny my knee breeches were twitching. I had a lot to worry about. If I got thrown out of the palace by the Venetian aristocrats who thought me a commoner, I would probably get stoned to death by the populace who mistook me for an aristocrat.

As we motored up the Grand Canal, I waved to the watching people and screamed, "*Vive la République*," and as we turned into the Canale di Cannaregio, where the palace was, I yelled, "*Vive la roi*." But when we touched the dock, I found to my dismay that I was two hours too early. Nobody was in costume, and the only people around the palace at that hour were working men being ordered about by the excited host. I casually sauntered in and walked up to the first wall, where I sat down inconspicuously under a Tiepolo fresco.

But I didn't sit there long. Don Carlos came storming around the corner. "Who are you?" he said angrily.

"Louis the Fourteenth," I answered weakly.

"Yes, but who are you?"

I told him my name and he yelled, "You weren't invited. Get out of my house."

"But you said it was all right to come at eight o'clock," I said.

"Out, out, get out of my house," he cried, and then rushed away to get reinforcements.

I ran upstairs and ducked into the first open room I saw, slamming the door behind me. It was pitch black in the room—and suddenly I heard the rustling of costumes. When I turned on the light I found two *Life* photographers and two *Life* researchers hiding under the bed.

All of us were in a bad spot. The room we had chosen was right next to Don Carlos's bedroom and he had to go through it to wash his hands.

We couldn't leave and we couldn't stay.

"To the window," yelled one of the researchers, and we all ran to the window and huddled on the balcony, closing the curtains behind us. Don Carlos entered five minutes later and went into his bedroom to get dressed. Every time he heard a cheer, he came to the balcony and waved to the people below, while the five of us froze tightly together. For two hours we didn't move and didn't speak, except for one of the photographers, who kept muttering, "A curse on this house. A curse on this house."

Finally, Don Carlos at ten o'clock went down to greet his guests and we staggered stiffly back into the room. From then on it was clear sailing, especially in my case, because as luck would have it, twenty guests turned up as Louis XIV.

I drank Don Carlos's wine, ate his lobster and chicken and danced with some of his beautiful guests. And as a democratic gesture, I waved to the mob in the square. By six o'clock I was tired and decided to leave. As I went out I thanked Don Carlos for a wonderful time.

"I'm glad you liked it," he said, apparently not recognizing which Louis XIV he was talking to. "It was awfully kind of you to come."